Cooklin's Garment Technology for Fashion Designers

2nd Edition

Cooklin's Garment Technology for Fashion Designers

2nd Edition

Steve Hayes,
John McLoughlin and
Dorothy Fairclough

A John Wiley and Sons, Ltd., Publication

This edition first published 2012
© S Hayes, J McLoughlin & D Fairclough

The first edition published 1997
© The Estate of Gerry Cooklin

Registered office
John Wiley & Sons Ltd, The Atrium, Southern Gate, Chichester, West Sussex, PO19 8SQ, United Kingdom

Editorial office
John Wiley & Sons Ltd, The Atrium, Southern Gate, Chichester, West Sussex, PO19 8SQ, United Kingdom

For details of our global editorial offices, for customer services and for information about how to apply for permission to reuse the copyright material in this book please see our website at www.wiley.com.

Library of Congress Cataloging-in-Publication Data

Hayes, Steve, Dr.
Cooklin's garment technology for fashion designers/Steve Hayes, John McLoughlin and Dorothy Fairclough. – 2nd ed.
p. cm.
Rev. ed. of: Garment technology for fashion designers/Gerry Cooklin.
Includes bibliographical references and index.
ISBN 9781405199742.

A catalogue record for this book is available from the British Library.

ISBN 9781405199742 (pbk); ISBN 9781119952466 (ebk);
ISBN 9781119952473 (ebk); ISBN 9781119952480 (ebk)

Set in 10pt Sabon LT Std by Aptara Inc., New Delhi, India
Printed in Italy by Printer Trento Srl

TABLE OF CONTENTS

PREFACE – ABOUT THIS REVISED EDITION

John and I revised *Introduction to Clothing Manufacture* on behalf of Gerry's estate and his publisher a few years ago and we are privileged to be asked to again provide a revised and updated version of his work with our 2nd edition of *Garment Technology for Fashion Designers*. To do this we needed to expand the team with the addition of 'Ms Garment Technology' herself, Dorothy Fairclough, thus allowing us to present a book which sticks to Gerry's original style but gives the fashion design student in the 21st century a useful overview of the technical aspects to fashion product development. Whilst it is true to say that the globalisation of the fashion industry has had a major impact on the distribution of roles between manufacturer and retailer many of the fundamentals of garment technology applicable to the design and development of fashion products have remained constant. The need for the designer to understand the impact of design decisions on production lead times and overall product costs is in fact of greater importance the more the marketing and design operations are decoupled from those of manufacturing and distribution. What we hope to provide with this edition is the technical knowhow to enhance the design, development and creation of fashion products and to minimise the disruptive impact of unsuitable, ill-conceived and poorly managed ideas fixed at the design stage but realised – and accounted for – during the creation phase. Three of the central themes covered in this edition are direct materials utilisation and labour costs, garment and textile technology and the operation of the product development department. These are all necessary areas for the designer/product developer to understand if they are to deliver product to the right price, to the right quality, at the right time and right for the targeted consumer.

Steven Hayes

ACKNOWLEDGEMENTS

Much of the original material from the 1st edition is still applicable today and has been re-used, therefore our thanks are extended to the machinery manufacturers, their agents and other organisations who provided the technical material and permission to reproduce illustrations of their products and exhibits for the 1st edition and also to those who have helped by providing technical images and details specifically for this revised version. Thanks especially to:

Paula Wren, Manchester Metropolitan University for the creation of the design specifications used in Chapter 14.

Caroline Hertz, Manchester Metropolitan University for her help in understanding the Product Development Process.

David Mellett, Matalan Ltd, UK for his advice on all aspects of garment manufacture.

PART 1

THE COMMERCIAL DESIGNER

CHAPTER 1

The Designer's Role within Product Development and Manufacture

The title "Fashion Designer" includes not only those who work at couture level, but also those involved in mass production at all price levels of the market. The well known named designers who design at couture level are of course in the minority; their garments are produced in small numbers in workrooms. Many of these designers will also be involved in creating diffusion ranges which although still exclusive will be more widely available and therefore will be considered to be mass produced. The vast majority of designers are involved in the creation of designs at all the other levels of the market: for the many high street stores, labels and other outlets. These garments are produced in even greater number.

All designers, including those operating at couture level, should understand the market, and the consumer, be aware of sizing, quality and costs relating to fabrics, trimmings and production. In addition those designing for the mass market need to be aware of catwalk trends and be able to adapt them for the high street. This book is aimed at the majority of designers creating styles at all levels of mass production.

The role of the designer may vary significantly depending on the requirements of the company but may operate thus: the designer is employed by the company producing the garments and will work closely with the buyer and merchandising team from the retail company from whom the merchandise will ultimately be sold, and as such is closely linked with the sales team. Both the buyer and the designer will be researching the same fashion forecasting sites and other sources of inspiration in order to put together a range of garments. Trends will be identified and utilised to suit the target market of that particular company. The buyer will often give the designer a brief which defines the types of garment which are to be included in the range and this will be influenced by previous seasons' sales.

In addition to researching key trends including garment shapes, colours and fabrics the designer should also have an awareness of market trends and competitors. A design pack is often produced to feed through to the product development team. This – and other types of visual communication – has become increasingly important as manufacturing is likely to be taking place in an overseas location and the product development team may be UK based or they too may be based overseas. It is the product developer's role to interpret and develop designs.

The buyer may initially select designs from an image. Then samples will be produced – this may take place in the UK or in the country where large scale production is to take place. Very detailed specifications are necessary to ensure that samples are correctly produced and to avoid costly mistakes. These include technical sketches, size charts, making details, fabric details and production details.

The role can vary depending on the level of the market, but also between companies. How the designer fits into the process of producing garments will depend on company size. In larger companies the designer will work in conjunction with a product development team whereas in a smaller company the role can encompass at least some of the product development role. The designer may produce the first pattern for the garment but often there is a pattern cutter who will perform this task. The designer manages the range construction to ensure that the samples are produced in line with the original concept. In some cases it is expected that the design of the fabric print is included in the remit. Multi-skilling has become increasingly important.

The designer cannot ignore the technical aspects of garment production even if there are others who are responsible for these areas. Many production problems can be avoided if these factors are taken into account during the design process.

GARMENT TECHNOLOGY

Technology has been defined as a technical method of achieving a practical purpose, but its original Greek root meaning is the systematic treatment of an art. This latter meaning is apt for the clothing industry because garment design is a goal oriented art form which requires technology to convert it into a finished product.

Clothing technology is a broad based subject because it combines a number of individual technologies, with each making a specialised contribution to the production of clothing. For the designer and pattern cutter, these technologies can be divided into two groups:

(1) Need to know: These are the technologies which are directly related to the work of designers and pattern cutters, and it is imperative that they have a practical understanding of the essentials of each particular subject.
(2) Good to know: This group covers the other technologies which are part of a modern clothing factory but are not of direct concern for designing and pattern cutting. However, the senior members of the design team should have some understanding of these technologies because it will improve their orientation within the working environment.

FOR THE DESIGNER AND PATTERN CUTTER

All clothing factories have a specific technological capability which has been built around the production of a particular category of garments. The levels of technology vary from factory to factory, even between those producing the same garment at similar time standards. Irrespective of the levels of operation, it is essential that the designer and pattern cutter both work according to the given framework and when possible, exploit it to its fullest extent.

With regard to the applications of technology, for the designer it is mainly a question of what the factory can do and knowing the extent of the permissible variations. The pattern cutter also has to know what the factory can do, but also to know how it is done and what is required to do it. These factors have to be incorporated into the garment pattern, plus all the standard technological processes which the average garment undergoes during making up.

Where does the interaction of the designer and pattern cutter with the factory's technology start? It starts with both of them learning and understanding the factory's technological resources and capabilities. This is vital for a full and efficient involvement on their part. It is inefficient to invest time in developing a design and pattern and then discovering that the factory is not equipped to perform one or more of the operations required.

Whether the company is prepared to invest in a new item of machinery or equipment is a commercial decision based on whether the acquisition will have a restricted use during one season only or whether it has a range of other possible applications. If the item is going to be limited to an unknown number of garments during one season only, it is back to the drawing board for the designer and pattern cutter.

The sample room is usually equipped with machinery which covers regular operations only, because it is costly to have high-tech machines which are only used occasionally in the sample room. When there are new samples which require operations beyond the scope of the sample room machinery, these operations should be performed in the factory and not "mocked up" in the sample section. The factory is where the garments will be produced and special operations should be validated there. It is important that the sample room produces garments which incorporate the relevant technology, and this means working closely with the factory. It is possible to improvise many special operations in the sample room with time and skilled labour, but this is not the situation in the factory. So the people responsible have to ensure that sample garments can be mass produced by utilising as much as possible of the available technology.

CHAPTER 2

The Designer and Garment Costs – The Commercial Designer

A garment design does not exist in a vacuum but is the end product of a chain of activities which can be said to start with the production of textile fibres. Various authorities have estimated that the time span between fibre production and the garment sampling stage can be as long as between six to eight months but as short as six to eight weeks for "fast fashion" items. For the clothing manufacturer, the internal chain of activities starts some time before the forthcoming season's materials are available because the company has to have some firmed-up ideas of what it intends doing before selecting materials.

The internal chain usually starts with the marketing/sales department doing some formal evaluation of historical sales performance to evaluate what the market sector served by the company could be looking for and at what prices. Parallel to this, the design team has researched trends in both fabric and garment styles through such channels as online trend bureaux, trade shows and street trends (along with some comparative shopping). Marketing and design put their heads together and start formulating the framework of the sample collection. Fabrics and trimmings are selected and pre-ordered, the designer starts to prepare the core designs, which will represent the central theme of the collection with a clear market orientation and brand identity if needed. Core designs, when approved, will be the basis for developing planned groups of variations. The pre-sales design room processes are shown in Figure 2.1.

In this context, garment design tends more toward a goal directed planning process because apart from developing the appeal factors of each design, the designer also has to take into account the many technical and commercial factors involved – this process is then often referred to as product development. So when designs have been approved and materials delivered, the design team has to become involved with the production of sample garments.

THE DESIGNER AND GARMENT COSTS

Under a free enterprise system it is accepted by the business world that money is the name of the game, and the clothing industry is no exception. The success of designs produced by a manufacturer can only be judged by the colour printed on the company's bank statement at the end of a season: red or black. There are many factors which can influence profitability, but in normal circumstances profitability originates to a large extent in the design section.

The Framework

Where does it all start for the designer? The answer is a combination of two factors:

- Market specialisation, and
- The average garment concept.

This linking of these two factors provides the designer with a reasonably accurate basis for initial cost estimates.

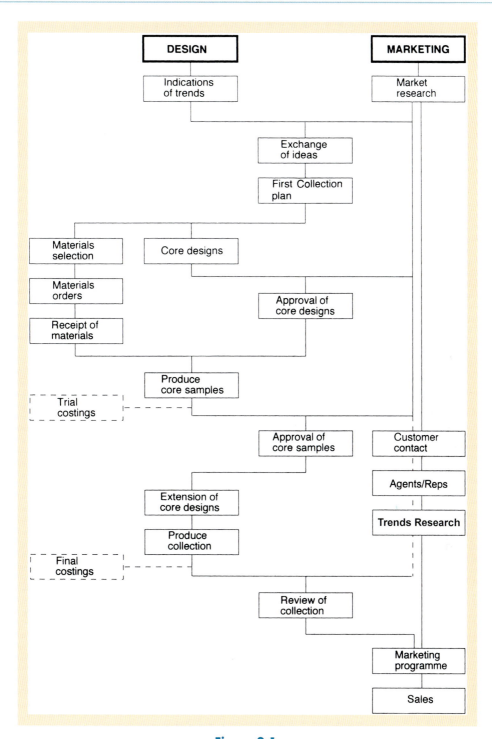

Figure 2.1.

Market Specialisation

The clothing industry is divided into sectors according to garment types, and within each sector there are subdivisions or sections based primarily on price. For example, one sector could be women's separates, with the sections having prices ranging from very cheap to highly expensive. The prices reflect not only the manufacturing costs and fashion content of the products but the brand equity associated with them.

The majority of clothing manufacturers concentrate on serving and expanding their share of a specific section within a sector. As a result, they accumulate a great deal of expertise regarding the suitability of products, prices and production demands. Knowing this, the company is able to break down its average ex-factory price into the main components, such as materials, labour, overheads and profit. The results of this analysis provide the designer with an accurate indication of what can be invested in an average garment in terms of materials and labour. The proportions between these two cost factors can vary from style to style, but their total has to be on, or very close to, the target in order that a new sample will be able to slot into the correct price bracket.

The Average Garment Concept

Most production units, irrespective of the production system employed, are built around the average garment concept where this term refers to a typical garment produced by the unit. This typical garment has an acceptable work content and the balance between the various groups of operations is reflected in the staffing and equipment of the unit. This type of factory would have the capability to handle a reasonable range of cloth and/or styling variations without serious modifications regarding staff, machinery and layout. However, in order to be more responsive to the market factories can be arranged with several independent production lines, which can be modified to cope with higher degrees of change in fabric and style with minimal disruption to the overall running of the factory.

The average garment concept is very widely used because of the production commonalities which exist between garments of the same type. In practice this means that regardless of individual styling, nearly every garment produced goes through the same standard operations. For example, the common operations for a unit producing skirts could be: overlocking, dart-sewing, closing side seams, zip setting, preparing and setting waistbands, top and under-pressing operations, finishing and inspection procedures.

It is important that production people communicate with the designer regarding the times for each group of operations in an average garment produced by the factory. With knowledge of these times and the average garment concept, the designer and technical staff can make amendments to the original garment design without detracting from original design concept. This ensures operations required will fit into the production balance of the factory.

Whilst nobody expects a fashion designer to be an expert in garment costing, designers must be aware of their influence on costs. Garments have to be evaluated for costs at the sampling stage because making samples without regard to price is often futile. So when necessary, the designer and pattern cutter have to modify designs and patterns so as to bring a new sample into the correct price framework.

THE GARMENT COSTING

Also known as the bill of materials, the garment costing details the costs of every item attributable to the production of a particular garment. The sum of these costs plus the profit margin is the selling price which the company will quote to customers. Alternatively, the reverse is true, where a customer is only prepared to pay a certain amount for a product. The manufacturer must reverse engineer the product from here to ensure they set production costs that allow them to achieve their desired profit margin. Whilst each company has its own method of preparing costings, generally the components of a costing are grouped under four headings: direct materials, direct labour, factory overhead and general overhead.

Direct Materials

Direct materials are all the materials and trimmings which go into the construction and finish of the garment. Typically, these materials could include fabric, lining, interlining, buttons, zips, pads, tapes, labels, tickets, hangers and packaging materials, etc.

Direct Labour

This covers the cost of all the labour directly involved in producing the garment and could include cutting, fusing, sewing operation, special machine operations, pressing, finishing, inspection and packing. Labour of all types and grades has a direct overhead which includes holiday pay, sick pay, fringe benefits, etc, and the statutory payments made by the employer for each employee. This is usually expressed as a percentage of salary and when this percentage is added to the employee's wage, it becomes the basis for calculating direct labour costs.

Factory Overhead

There are different methods of calculating the factory overhead, but most of them use a combination of the following three elements:

(1) Indirect labour: This covers every person in the factory who does not directly perform a production operation, such as managers, supervisors, engineers, store personnel, clerks, maintenance staff, porters, canteen staff, security and cleaners, etc.
(2) Expenses: Included in this element is every fixed and variable expense incurred in operating the factory, such as rent, rates, utilities, insurance, depreciation, maintenance and the various types of energy consumption/generation required by a clothing factory.
(3) Indirect materials: Also known as consumables, this element contains all the materials not directly connected to the make-up of a garment. Some of the typical items involved are office materials, spare parts, marker paper and maintenance materials.

The total of these three elements is the factory overhead and because it cannot be conveniently applied to specific cost units, it is generally expressed as a percentage of the direct labour costs. For example, using the arbitrary figures below, the costs for a given period are:

Direct labour	£38 000 (including direct overhead)
Factory overhead	£45 600

The factory overhead is 120% of the cost of direct labour. From this, it is simple to calculate the cost of one minute's work for every production operator:

Labour rate per hour	£5.93 (UK minimum wage for over 21s as of October 2010)
Factory overhead at 120%	£7.12
Total cost	£13.05
Cost per work minute	£0.22

Therefore the price of an operation is the rate per minute multiplied by the time allowed for the operation.

General Overhead

The general overhead comprises all the labour costs and expenses which are incurred in running the company, such as management, marketing, finance, insurance, warehousing, rent and utilities. The design department costs are usually allocated to this component.

Again, because of the practical difficulties of apportioning this component to specific cost units, it is expressed as a percentage of the total for direct labour, factory overhead and direct materials, as in this example, where all the costs are for the same period:

Direct materials	£114 000
Direct labour	£38 000
Factory overheads at 120%	£45 600
Total	£197 600
General overhead	£88 920

Therefore, conveniently, the general overhead is 45% of all the other costs. So the framework of a garment costing would be the sum total of these four components.

An example of a garment costing is shown in Figure 2.2; the figures are for demonstration purposes only. Whilst the method of computation, detail, terminology and format can vary from company to company, the primary objectives of the costing are always the same: how much does the garment cost to produce?

Garment Costing

Style #	Comp. #			Market	Description
6114	HC 20 664			Domestic	Straight Coat
Season	**Phase**			**Size range**	**Unit**
Winter	2			36-42	A1

Item	Description	Supplier	Quan.	Price	Unit cost
Fabric	100%wool - 4608	Star mills	2.6	9.4	24.44
Lining	Satin - 856	Lintex	2.4	3.8	9.12
Interlining	w311-a	Fusemat	0.9	2.9	2.61
Buttons	1142-#40	Fladon	6	0.2	1.20
Pads	Raglan - 16 (pair)	A Slek	1	0.65	0.65
Thread	120's pp	Gutterman	200	0.0015	0.30
Label	brand	stock	1	0.08	0.08
Size label	UK	stock	1	0.07	0.07
Care label	100% wool/ dry clean	stock	1	0.1	0.10
Ticket	brand - fine	stock	1	0.12	0.12
Hanger	T6	Hangetti	1	0.4	0.40
Packaging	coat bag - 8	Plast pac	1	0.25	0.25

Production	Min.		Price	Cost	Materials	39.34
Cutting	6		0.26	1.56	**Production**	22.54
Fusing	2		0.22	0.44	**Gen. o/ heads**	29.87
Sewing	55		0.24	13.2	**Total cost**	91.75
Specials	6		0.22	1.32	**Profit**	15.00
Under pressing	6		0.22	1.32	**Commission**	3.50
Top pressing	11		0.22	2.42	**Total cost**	110.25
Finishing	4		0.22	0.88	**Selling Price**	110.00
Inspection	4		0.24	0.96	**Prepared by**	sgh
Packing	2		0.22	0.44		
Total	**96**		Total	**22.54**	**Date**	24th Nov

Figure 2.2.

The Designer's Role

The preparation of a garment costing is usually the work of a costing clerk who collates all the relevant information and calculates money values. Before the costing process starts, the design needs to be checked and approved as to the basic viability, within cost, for production by the design team and production/technical personnel. Skilled marker planners can reduce materials requirements, and production engineers can accurately analyse work content, but if the sample garment is carrying excessive costs of materials and/or labour, there is very little that these people can do to make the garment an acceptable proposition without the input and collaboration of the designer. So the designer should never be designing in isolation and is a key member of the product development team.

CHAPTER 3

Pattern Cutting and Materials Utilisation

This chapter examines the critical influence of the garment pattern on the pivotal activities in a clothing factory. There is no doubt that pattern cutting, whether performed manually or with a CAD system, is the most important technical process in the production of clothing. Apart from effective design interpretation, the pattern cutter has a major responsibility to provide the basis for the most efficient usage of materials.

MATERIALS UTILISATION

Various research projects have established that approximately 85% of the materials purchased for garment production are in the finished garment, with the remainder for one reason or another ending up as waste. This figure is called the materials utilisation percentage and it is a crucial cost factor in the price of a garment. Materials generally comprise about 50% of the cost price of a garment with labour representing approximately 20%. So an improvement of, say, 5% in materials utilisation is worth far more than a 5% reduction in production time. Whilst the pattern cutter cannot personally prevent excess materials usage in the cutting room, there are a number of procedures which can be employed to ensure that the garment pattern makes the minimum possible demands on materials requirements. These procedures are grouped together under the heading of pattern engineering.

Pattern Engineering

The overall objectives of pattern engineering are to improve the utilisation factor of a garment pattern through prudent modifications which do not degrade the design integrity. A line has to be drawn between the enhancement of materials utilisation and the maintenance of the design objectives. If the sweep of a fully flared dress is reduced by four to five centimetres or the depth of a skirt waist band is decreased by two or three millimetres, would these modifications make any material difference to the final appearance and fit of the garment? If pattern modifications are planned, they should be considered with a large measure of common sense.

The central procedures of pattern engineering are pattern accuracy, major modifications and making-up allowances.

Pattern Accuracy

Pattern accuracy is a fundamental subject. It is said, with justification, that apart from cutting mistakes, the accuracy of a pattern cutter can be judged by the amount and size of the cuttings found on the sewing room floor. Production operators are not supposed to be cutters. If they have to remove surpluses from components because of incorrect pattern alignments or erroneous allowances, then only the pattern cutter is responsible. Apart from the wasted materials, the production operators are to some extent prevented from doing the work they are engaged to do, so this situation is a twofold loss for the company. It can be eliminated to a large extent by greater precision on the part of the pattern cutter.

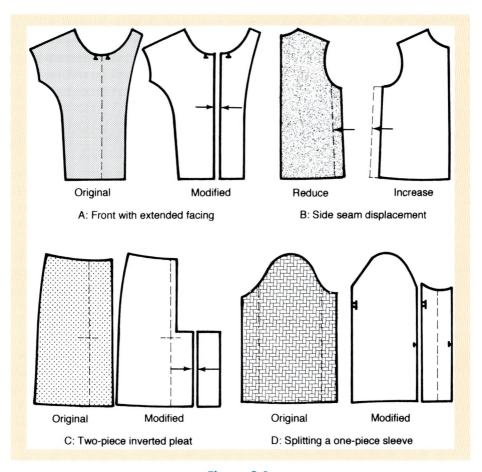

| Original | Modified | Reduce | Increase |

A: Front with extended facing   B: Side seam displacement

| Original | Modified | Original | Modified |

C: Two-piece inverted pleat   D: Splitting a one-piece sleeve

Figure 3.1.

Major Modifications

These modifications could include seam displacements, slight reductions in flare, splitting very large components, separate instead of extended facings, etc. Some examples are shown in Figure 3.1. These, and other similar major modifications, require a pragmatic type of flexibility from the designer and pattern cutter because, design considerations apart, every saving in materials is a potential advantage for the company.

It is worth remembering that whilst many of today's consumers are design and quality literate, they are still not clothing technicians, so a small element of "bluff" is permissible.

Making-up Allowances

This covers seam and hem allowances and facing widths. According to an American survey, seam and hem allowances can together account for approximately 5.5% of the material used for the actual garment. So it is up to the pattern cutter to ensure that all these allowances are the practical minimum possible.

Seams

The most important properties of a seam are strength and flexibility and these are determined by a number of technical factors plus the characteristics of the fabric and the width of the seam allowance. Some of the more important technical factors are examined in Chapter 8, whilst a more comprehensive treatment can be found in Tyler (2008).

The width of seam allowances is primarily decided by the characteristics of the fibre to be sewn and the type of seam being sewn. In order to establish an appropriate background for the examination of these two factors, the construction elements of the most commonly used seam will be analysed. This seam, referred to as a superimposed seam, is constructed by sewing two components together along one edge of each piece (Figure 3.2), and the seam is usually pressed open.

Over many years, the clothing industry has proved that for regularly constructed fabrics, the optimal seam margin for assembly seams is 1 cm. This width combines three important elements:

(1) Transverse strength (Figure 3.3) – In this context, strength refers to the ability of the seam to withstand reasonable pressures at angles to its length without spreading open excessively.
(2) Handling The width is sufficient for the presser to open the seam easily by hand when pressing it open.
(3) For operator controlled seaming there has to be an adequate margin between the right hand side of the pressure foot and the edge of the seam being sewn. When using a regular presser foot this margin enables the operator to visually control seam width (Figure 3.4).

It is generally accepted that loosely constructed materials require slightly larger seam allowances than those for more tightly woven fabrics. There are no

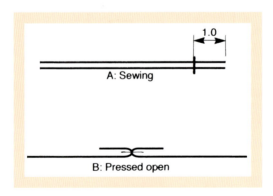

Figure 3.2.

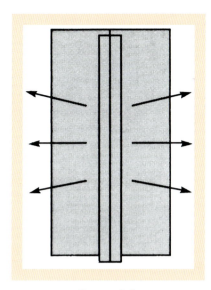

Figure 3.3.

rules governing this additional allowance, but in many cases, 2 or 3 mm would be sufficient. If in doubt, it is worth testing seam strength before making a decision, because wider seam allowances are not necessarily required for every type of loosely constructed fabric if the crimp percentage is high in the yarns or the fibres give the yarns greater frictional properties. The allowances for the main type of standard seams are given here.

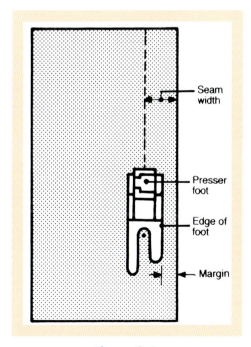

Figure 3.4.

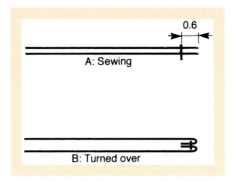

Figure 3.5.

Edges

These are enclosed seams which are typically used for the edges of collars, lapels and flaps, etc. For profile or jig-sewing a seam width of 5 mm is used, and for operator controlled edge sewing 6 mm. In both cases, if the sewing machine also has an edge trimming action, an additional 2 mm is necessary.

Knits

Garments made from knits are nearly always assembled by overlock or safety-stitch machines and the basic seam allowance is derived from the bight of the machine to be used. The bight refers to the finished seam width produced by the machine and to this an allowance of 2 or 3 mm has to be added for edge trimming.

Lap Felled Seams

Commonly used for jeans and similarly styled garments, the seam allowance is determined by the needle gauge of the machine to be used. The needle gauge is the measurement between the centres of the two needles and the seam allowance is calculated as follows:

1.5 (needle gauge) + 1 mm

For example, given a needle gauge of 8 mm, the seam allowance would be:

12 mm + 1 mm = 13 mm

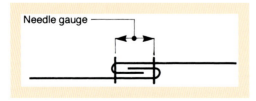

Figure 3.6.

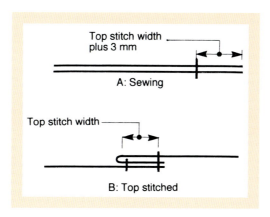

Figure 3.7.

Top Stitched Seams

The two elements which determine the sewing allowances for these seams are the width of the top stitching and the thickness of the material. For very light weight materials, the seam margin is the width of the top stitching plus 2 or 3 mm (Figure 3.7). If the edges of the seam are to be overlocked, an addition of 2 or 3 mm is necessary.

On heavy materials this method would produce a thick, stiff seam and this can be remedied by using different allowances on the two components which are to be joined and top stitched. For the top component, which is top stitched; the sewing allowance is the width of the top stitch minus 3 mm. The allowance on the under component is the top stitch width plus 3 mm. Figure 3.8 illustrates the application of these allowances and it can be seen that the resultant seam construction would be thinner and more pliable than if the two components had the same seam widths.

Other Seam Types

An enormous variety of seam constructions is used in the clothing industry and it is beyond the scope of this book to examine the allowances for all of them. Some of the allowances can be pre-determined by the apparatus employed to construct

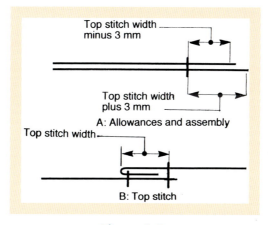

Figure 3.8.

the seam, whilst others are derived from the width of a material which is to be applied to, or inserted in, a seam. It is always worth checking carefully what exactly is required and, if there is any doubt, experimentation is advisable.

Final Word on Seam Allowances

Modern sizing technology ensures that the majority of consumers can purchase garments which do not require alterations to girths except possibly, skirt and trouser waist bands. Consequently there is no real practical reason to include allowances on the pattern for increasing the girths of body garments. Wider than necessary seam allowances are sometimes used for skirts and dresses, and these seams are supposedly an indication of garment quality as perceived by the consumer. This approach is perfectly acceptable if it is company policy, as long as the company understands that these seams are an additional cost factor.

Hems

This refers to the turn-ups on the lower extremities of body garments, skirts, trousers and sleeves etc, and the same considerations apply to both the top cloth and lining. The guiding principle for this group of allowances is that they should be just sufficient for their purpose but no more. There is no need to allow for the possible lengthening of a garment because normal height differences are usually catered for by the standard short, medium and tall size ranges. It is impossible to provide hem allowances that will cover every possible eventuality of height variations.

A garment or sleeve hem, apart from the finish which it imparts, also gives a certain amount of weight and stability to the hem line. Both these elements have a beneficial influence on the finished appearance of a garment, thus contributing to its overall quality. Different garment types have varying requirements as regards acceptable hem widths and the general industrial practice is:

Body garments – outerwear and light clothing: Garment hems 4 cm. Sleeve hems 3.5–4 cm.
Trousers and skirts – outerwear and light clothing: Hems 3.5 cm.
Woven blouses and shirts – Hem width gross 1.2 cm.

Both the body and sleeve hems are usually double turned by standard folders. Figure 3.9 shows this hem formation and the difference between the gross and net widths. If the sleeve is not finished with an attached or extended cuff, the gross turn-up width is 2.2 cm.

Cut Knits (for example, T-shirts and jumper garment hems and sleeve hems 2.0 cm)

Manufacturers of cut knits have standard single turn folders (Figure 3.10) on their hemming machines and the pattern has to have an allowance which matches the folder plus 2 or 3 mm for edge trimming. As an alternative a bottom cover stitch may be used on the 2.0 cm allowance.

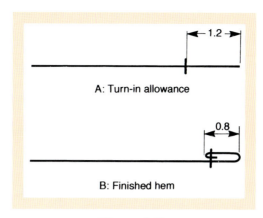

Figure 3.9.

Flared Hems

In all cases when the body or sleeve hem is flared, the standard hem allowance should be reduced in order to ensure a flat lying turn-in. For very flared hem lines, such as that of a circular skirt, the allowance can be as little as 8 mm plus 2–3 mm for overlocking.

Lining Hems

There are two types of hem allowances for linings and the type used depends on whether the lining hem is sewn to the garment or is left open:

Sewn hems – The allowance for sewn lining hems is derived directly from the hem widths of the body and sleeve. No savings can be made, apart from not exaggerating shrinkage and ease allowances.

Open hems (Figure 3.11) – These are mostly used for flared garments because the lining hem sweep is usually less than that of the garment as the lining only needs to have sufficient sweep to allow for a comfortable stride length.

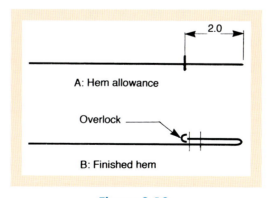

Figure 3.10.

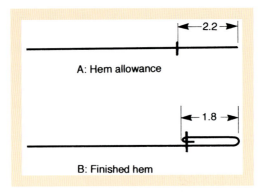

Figure 3.11.

Facing Widths

For practical purposes, the width of a front facing depends to a large extent on the direction of the buttonholes in relation to the front edge. There are two standard directions:

Vertical – Where the buttonholes are parallel to the front edge.
Horizontal – Where the buttonholes are at right angles to the front edge.

The factors which govern the calculation of the relevant facing widths are given here.

Vertical Buttonholes (Figure 3.12A)

Vertical buttonholes are nearly always located on the centre front line of single breasted garments; typical examples are blouses and shirts. If the garment has an attached or extended placket down the forepart, the facing width is the same as the placket plus whatever allowances are needed for assembly and finishing. This calculation also applies to garments having an inset placket, such as polo shirts.

Horizontal Buttonholes (Figure 3.12B)

Facings for garments with horizontal buttonholes can, for demonstration purposes, be divided into two sections:

Section 1 from the shoulder to the top buttonhole
Section 2 from the top buttonhole down to the hem.

The details which have to be taken into account when calculating the width of the lower section (section 2) are:

- The distance between the eye of the buttonhole and the front edge, usually equal to half the diameter of the button plus 5 or 6 mm.
- The length of the buttonhole itself, which is based on the diameter and thickness of the button.

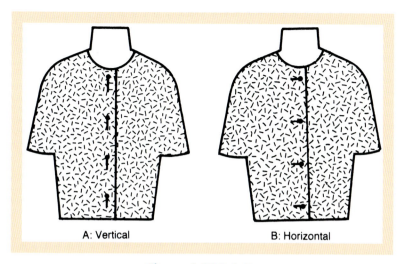

A: Vertical   B: Horizontal

Figure 3.12A & B.

- An allowance from the end of the buttonhole to the inside edge of the facing, which needs to be sufficient to allow for blindstitching and lining setting.

These details are illustrated in Figure 3.13 and their total provides the width of the lower section.

If the garment is unlined and not blindstitched, apart from an allowance for overlocking, the facing should extend past the end of the buttonhole so as to

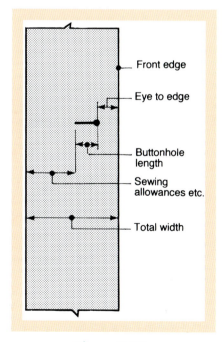

Front edge

Eye to edge

Buttonhole length

Sewing allowances etc.

Total width

Figure 3.13.

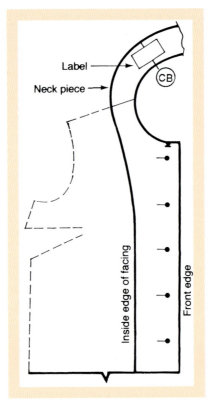

Figure 3.14.

enable the foot of the buttonhole machine to clamp down on to a flat surface. A total of 12–15 mm would be adequate for these two allowances.

The width and run of the facing's upper section are based on whether a label is attached to the back neck piece. It is preferable for the combined inside edge of the neck piece and facing to be a smooth, continuous line for its whole length. If a label is positioned on the neck piece, the width of the neck piece has to be sufficient to contain the label plus a small margin all round. Thus the total net width of the neck piece provides the start of the inside edge line which runs down to the lower section (Figure 3.14). Where the label is attached to the body lining, a net back piece width of 4 cm is sufficient for most purposes.

Cut Trimmings

Other areas of materials utilisation include trimmings which have to be cut, as against trim which is purchased ready-made. The two most widely used cut trimmings are fusible interlinings and linings, and as together, they represent a significant cost component of garments, the patterns for these materials also have to contain only the practical minimum possible.

Fusible Interlinings

Pattern cutting for fusible interlinings is examined in Chapter 6; here we deal with the pattern engineering aspects. The effect of fusible interlinings on the finished appearance of a garment can be seen, whereas the fusible interlinings themselves cannot be seen. This allows for some creative pattern engineering to be applied.

Interlocking Components

On many garments, the fusible interlinings for some of the components are cut from the same material. This provides an excellent opportunity for the pattern cutter to maximise the potential for tightly interlocking components, which has two benefits:

Waste is decreased because the spaces between components are reduced or completely eliminated.

When, say, two components are completely interlocked by means of a common line, then only one line instead of two has to be cut to separate components – a small but worthwhile saving of labour.

Unlike pattern modifications to top cloth components, there is only one question to be asked regarding the form of a pattern for a fusible interlining:

If the fusible interlining is not intended to completely cover the cloth component, then is the form of the edges of the fusible interlining – which do not have to align with the edges of the component – important?

The following examples show different applications of interlocking. The first is a demonstration of the principles involved.

Example 1

These are two standard components which have to be cut from an omnidirectional, non-woven fusible interlining:

(1) Lapel facing – this covers the lapel section only and extends for 2 or 3 cm over the crease line.
(2) Under collar – cut to the exact shape of the cloth under collar.

Figure 3.15A shows how these two components were originally positioned in the cutting marker, with the resultant waste plus the necessity for cutting two lines in order to separate them. After modifications to the lapel fusible, the interlocking of the two components is illustrated in Figure 3.15B. This new pattern arrangement has resulted in a reduction of waste and one common cutting line between the two pieces.

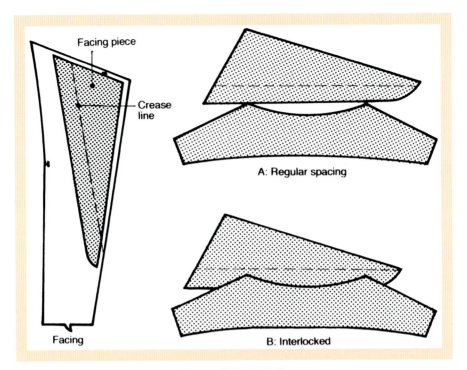

Facing piece

Crease line

Facing

A: Regular spacing

B: Interlocked

Figure 3.15A & B.

The line of the lapel fusible is a non-functional line and is distanced from the crease line only to ensure that the crease line is covered, with something to spare. Three changes have been made to this particular line:

(1) It has a small V notch in its upper section
(2) The curve of the collar's neck seam has been incorporated into part of its width
(3) Whilst the length has been slightly reduced and the form of the end has been changed, the piece still covers the top buttonhole.

These three modifications have not made the slightest difference to the functionality of the component but have produced changes for the better as regards materials usage and cutting time. Again fusible interlinings are not seen, so some "doctoring" of the non-functional lines is permissible, especially when this operation results in savings.

Example 2

Conventionally a partially fused front runs from the shoulder to the hem line and from a point on the armhole also to the hem line. The shoulder, armhole, neck and front edge lines are 100% functional, but the line from the armhole to the hem is non-functional. This particular line is really only a shaped line which connects a selected point on the armhole to a point on the hem line. The distance of this last point from the front edge only has to be sufficient to catch the

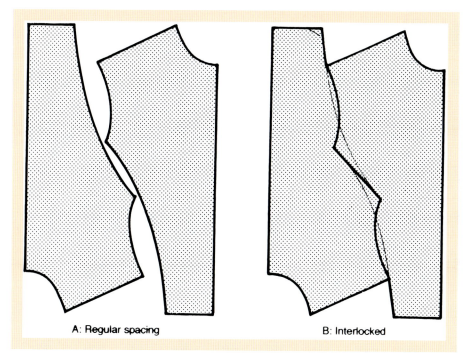

A: Regular spacing   B: Interlocked

Figure 3.16A & B.

blindstitching of the facing, which is generally about 2 cm from the gross inside edge of the facing itself.

Figure 3.16A shows the original positioning of a pair of these components in the cutting marker, with the ensuing waste and the need to cut two lines. Figure 3.16B illustrates the level of interlocking which can be achieved through rational pattern modifications. A reduction in waste and the elimination of one line are both brought about by pattern changes which have no influence on functionality.

General Considerations

Where possible these pieces should be of one length and one form only for all sizes. For example, if the seam allowance on both of the cloth sleeve underseams is, say 1 cm, the fact that the hem fusible will be a little too long or a little too short on some sizes is not particularly relevant because:

- excess length is easily disregarded by the operator who sews the underseam.
- the lack of a few millimetres at this position on the sleeve is of no real consequence.
- combining one length and one shape also has the advantage that the grading of this piece is eliminated and the cutting room is not required to separate different sizes.

Patterns for fusible interlining components have much potential for modifications which can result in worthwhile savings of materials and time. This is another important aspect of the pattern cutter's work.

Linings

Linings are also an important cost component and whilst the potential for pattern modifications is limited, there are some minor procedures which can enhance the utilisation of materials. A simple and convenient work-aid which can help the pattern cutter is to mark on his or her work table the standard width of the lining used by the factory. (A narrow, coloured adhesive tape is recommended for this purpose.) By using these marks the pattern cutter is able, at an early stage, to evaluate which pattern modifications would be viable. Some of the possible modifications are given here.

Skirt Linings

Conventionally, skirt lining patterns are positioned in cutting markers according to the warp grain line of the material. If folded lining is used, this pattern arrangement generally leads to a relatively high percentage of marker waste. All clothing industry professionals know that materials utilisation is higher on open materials than on folded materials, and linings are no exception.

An option which can be used on open lining, pattern length permitting, is to position the pattern component across the lining instead of down the length (Figure 3.17). Some purists might say that lining is stronger in its length than in its width. They are correct, but linings are firmly constructed materials and the weft direction is generally strong enough to withstand the regular pressures exerted on skirt linings. If necessary the side seams can be displaced from the hip line down. Positioning components across the fabric can also be used for trousers with knee length linings, again subject to pattern length.

Body Linings

Unlike fusible interlinings, body linings are seen and whilst this severely limits the possibilities of major pattern modifications, there are always opportunities for

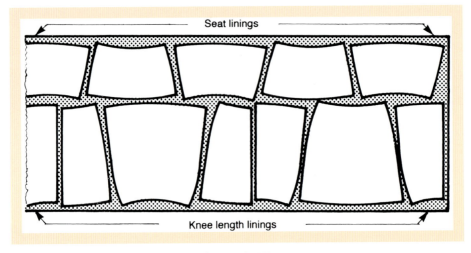

Figure 3.17.

improving materials utilisation. The two main components of a full lining are the body and the sleeve and the following examines what can be applied to both of them.

The Body: If the body lining patterns for a straight garment are being used to plan a cutting marker, there is always the possibility that displacing the side seams could lead to a more efficient marker. This particular displacement could take three different forms where a reasonable seam displacement of, say, 3 cm at each point is not exceeded:

(1) From zero at the armhole to a maximum of 3 cm at the hem
(2) From zero at the hem to a maximum of 3 cm at the armhole
(3) Displacing the entire length of the side seam up to 3 cm in either direction.

If the lining seam has been displaced at the armhole (Figure 3.18), then the lower section of armhole on the extended component should be nipped in order to indicate to the operator who tacks this area of the lining that the correct alignment is nip to seam and not seam to seam.

Displacing the seams of fitted linings should be avoided whenever possible but, if absolutely necessary, the displacements should be minimal – millimetres not centimetres – because different locations of waist suppression on the cloth and lining could lead to problems. On the body lining for a fitted coat the side seams can be displaced from the hip line down to the hem (Figure 3.19).

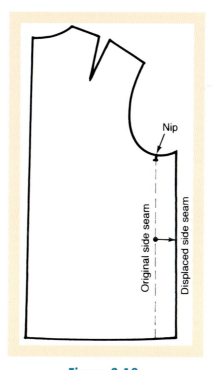

Figure 3.18.

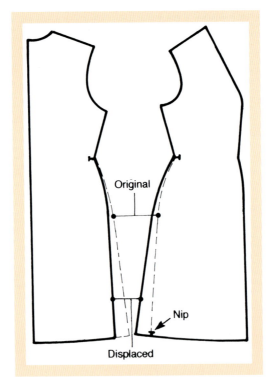

Figure 3.19.

The Sleeve: Patterns for sleeve linings allow for simple modifications because the major part of their length is concealed. These modifications fall into two categories:

(1) Joins – most companies accept that joins in the width of a sleeve lining are necessary in order to prevent excessive waste. When the pattern cutter sees that there is an advantage in joining a sleeve pattern, proper patterns for the joined parts should be prepared instead of relying on the marker planner to establish the join line, add seam allowances and mark sewing alignment nips.

(2) Seam displacements – these are made so that components will efficiently utilise the space available for them. A good example of seam displacements is those which can be applied to a standard, two-piece tailored sleeve. The practical options, shown below, all concern displacements of the hind arm seam because displacements of the forearm seam can cause problems due to the differences in seam locations.

Displacing the hind arm seams to increase the width of the top sleeve cuff and decrease that of the under sleeve, or vice versa. The points for this and other pivoting procedures are shown in Figure 3.20.

It is also possible to decrease the head width of the top sleeve and increase the width of the related section of the under sleeve. This is also performed by pivoting the pattern from the cuff and the result is shown in Figure 3.21A.

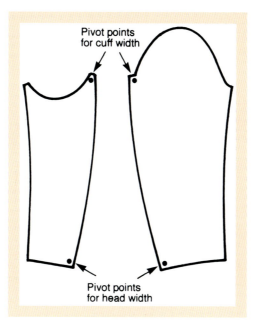

Figure 3.20.

Displacing the hind arm seams for their whole length, with the maximum displacement at any one point not exceeding 2.5 cm. This displacement does not have to be uniform for the entire length of the seam but can vary from top to bottom. Figure 3.21B shows an equidistant displacement of the hind arm seams

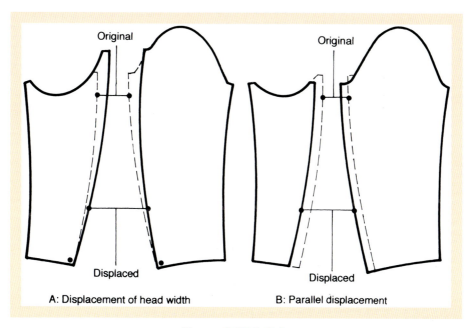

A: Displacement of head width   B: Parallel displacement

Figure 3.21A & B.

which is based on the principle that whatever is reduced from one seam is added exactly to the matching seam. If this type of displacement results in a wider top sleeve and a narrower under sleeve, then there will be an increase in the amount of top sleeve hind arm seam fullness which has to be eased into the hind arm seam of the under sleeve. Two sewing alignment notches along the seam would ensure the correct distribution of the fullness.

As stated at the start of this section, lining patterns do not present many opportunities for modification, but every gain, however small, is a plus for the company.

Computerised Cutting

If the samples and/or bulk work are to be cut by a CAM system, the patterns used for all materials should have a small modification made to their external corners in order to slightly reduce cutting time. The cutting blade of a computer controlled cutting head cannot turn through a sharp corner without disturbing a small area of the surrounding material. Consequently, most CAM systems use the following sequence for cutting corners:

(1) The first converging line of the corner is cut to its end.
(2) The blade is then automatically lifted out of the spread and swivelled to the required angle.

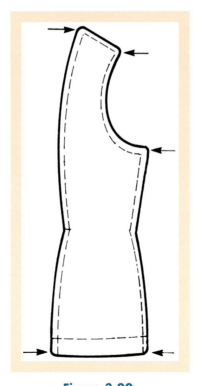

Figure 3.22.

(3) It is then plunged back into the lay and starts cutting the second convergent line of the corner. This lift and plunge sequence takes very little time in itself, but when it is used for the numerous sharp corners in a long lay, the time involved can be a significant proportion of the total time required to cut the lay.

The lift and plunge process can be eliminated by slightly rounding off all the sharp external corners of pattern components. As a result, the blade cuts round the corner in an uninterrupted instead of an interrupted action, thus saving time. For components having a seam allowance of 1 cm or more, a coin or disc with a diameter of about 1.5 cm can be used as a template for marking pattern corners. Figure 3.22 shows an example of a jacket panel with rounded off external corners.

CHAPTER 4

Garment Trimmings

In total all the trimmings used for a garment can be a substantial cost item and so their selection and use require careful consideration. Cost reductions made through improved materials utilisation can be negated by the resultant need for, or inappropriate selection of, trimmings.

LININGS

Garment linings have functional and consumer appeal objectives and this section will examine the principles involved, starting with the material itself.

Fibre Types and Properties

Natural fibres are rarely used to construct linings due to the high cost and some difficulties with imparting a suitable finish to the fabrics. Synthetic fibres are most widely accepted for garment linings, and the following describes the main properties of those which have the most widespread use in the clothing industry.

Viscose

Viscose is made from cellulose which is derived from wood pulp, and like most other synthetic fibres, it goes through a number of chemical and mechanical processes until the filaments are ready for spinning into yarns. Linings constructed from viscose fibres have strength, lustre, softness and an affinity for dyes.

Rayon

Originally rayon was produced as a cheap substitute for silk and the fibres were known as "artificial silk". Rayon linings have similar properties to those of viscose linings but are somewhat weaker.

Polyamide

Polyamide produces linings with excellent tensile strength and a relatively high degree of elasticity, and it takes dyestuffs very well. A drawback with polyamide linings is that some solvents used for dry cleaning can have a detrimental effect on the fabric.

Polyester

Polyester fibres are closely related to polyamides and linings made from polyester fibres have many similar properties. The first polyester linings had a tendency to soften when pressed with a hot iron, but fibres with a high melting point have since been developed and these withstand regular pressing temperatures.

Other than some polyamide linings, none of the linings made from these synthetic fibres are harmed by dry cleaning and they can be safely pressed up to a temperature of 170° C. Although some warp knitted linings are available, weaving is the predominant method of construction and three of the basic weaves are shown in Figure 4.1.

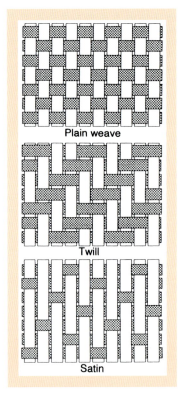

Figure 4.1.

Function and Consumer Appeal
Function
Garment linings have a number of functional purposes besides their main one which is to cover all or part of the interior surface of a garment. These other functions include the following:

- As linings have a sheer surface, putting on or taking off the garment is a smooth and simple action. Linings help to preserve the shape of skirts and trousers made from loosely constructed or stretchy materials. Garments such as dresses, skirts and trousers, made from more transparent fabrics, sometimes need areas making more opaque. Lining does this job well.
- Some types of outerwear materials have a tendency to cling to the body and this can spoil the silhouette of the garment. A layer of lining between the body of the wearer and the top cloth will usually eliminate this problem.
- Linings are often used to assist in the formation of design features on garments. For example, the difference in lengths between the body shell and the body lining creates the blouson effect.

Consumer Appeal

An important factor of consumer appeal is to present a garment whose inside has an attractive appearance. The surface and lustre properties of the lining have a considerable influence on this, and those properties for linings most widely used are:

Taffeta – a crisp fabric woven with a faint warp pattern which produces a shiny surface. These linings are generally piece-dyed which helps to soften them and make them able to withstand normal washing and dry cleaning processes.

Satin (sateen) – this lining is characterised by a smooth and highly lustrous surface and a dull back. Satin is the name of a weave pattern and all-cotton fabrics that were once constructed with this weave pattern were called sateen.

Sometimes other constructions are used such as:

Crepe – made from specially processed yarns, mostly viscose acetate, the finished surface of this lining has a minute and uniformly crinkled appearance.

Colour also plays an important role and linings with a woven, printed or embossed pattern can also enhance the aesthetic design of the garment as well as performing a functional role. Some large companies incorporate their logo in the weave pattern of their linings.

The Selection of Linings

This is not a simple matter because the properties of different linings overlap to a considerable extent and usually there is little difference in their prices. Apart from considering price, the designer should always work with reputable suppliers who can supply practical proof of the specific properties of their linings. Failing that, a sample length should be requested for trying out in the factory. As much consideration should be given to the selection of the lining as is given to the main fabric of the garment.

Practicalities

Making Up and Testing Linings

Lining materials fray easily and should be assembled with a suitable seam allowance; when enclosed they should not normally require neatening. However, where linings are not fully enclosed an edge neatening stitch type should be used. Although thread consumption is greater than on a regular sewing machine, the seam produced is superior. As with other aspects of garment production it advisable to under press seams as the lining is incorporated into the garment.

Lining Component Patterns

Grain line markings are as necessary for linings as they are for top cloth and fusible interlinings. They should match the grain lines of the relative cloth components, although this can be ignored for components such as sleeve linings and linings for skirts and trousers, which are sometimes cut across the piece instead of in the length.

Linings rarely have a pile direction and the up and down arrangement of the components for one size is a standard procedure in the industry. However, it is always safer to check this, especially with sateen, patterned or brushed finish linings. If the lining does have a definite direction, this has to be indicated on the pattern.

The number of notches on lining patterns should be kept to the minimum because every notch is a potential weak spot on the seams. In addition, if the notches fray out before sewing, the assembly operator will have to skirt round the frayed areas by sewing wider seams than those called for.

Despite the fact that linings are sometimes referred to as a secondary material, they have an important functional and consumer appeal role. Therefore the selection, patterns, cutting and making up of linings should receive the same levels of treatment as those accorded to the top cloth.

SECONDARY TRIMMINGS

Closures

Most garments require some form of working parts to open and close them and those parts which are not attached to the garment during its production have to be added in the finishing process. Typical closure systems are discussed here.

Buttons

Buttons and loops were first used to fasten clothing about 600 BC and with the development of the buttonhole in the 13th century buttons became the most widely used closure system for clothing of all types. Throughout the centuries buttons have been made from wood, precious metals and ceramics, many of which are collectors' items today. The modern button is mostly produced from plastic materials such as polyester, acrylic and polyvinyl resins, and they can be designed according to specific requirements (Figure 4.2). Garment buttons can serve two purposes:

(1) Utilitarian – this refers to buttons which are used to open and close garments and other design features where the wearer requires access combined with an element of security, for example the hip pocket on a trouser.
(2) Decorative – these are buttons which have a purely decorative function, for example a double-breasted jacket. Some of the buttons sewn on to the sleeve vents of tailored garments are of decorative value only, although at one time they had a functional purpose.

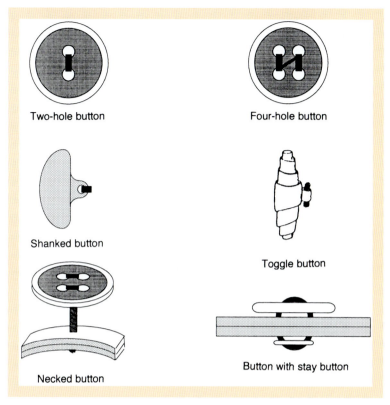

Two-hole button

Four-hole button

Shanked button

Toggle button

Necked button

Button with stay button

Figure 4.2.

Hooks and Eyes

This is a relatively simple closure system which is widely used for the top of zip openings on dresses, skirts, trousers and blouses. Hooks and eyes can be sewn on by hand or by a simple button sewing machine fitted with special clamps for the two working parts.

Hooks and Bars

These are metal closures which are used for trouser and skirt waist bands. Due to their construction, they have to be set whilst the garment is being assembled. If the factory specialises in the production of trousers and/or skirts, the sample room would usually be equipped with a manually operated device for attaching these parts (Figure 4.3). In the factory these machines are semi-automatic and powered by compressed air or electro-mechanical systems.

Press Studs

These can be made from plastic or metal and consist of two working parts, the male and female, which are locked together when subjected to a slight pressure. It is advisable to set press studs through two plies of material and with knitted fabrics a reinforcement strip between the two plies will prevent distortion.

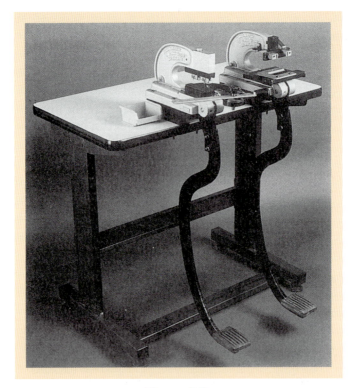

Figure 4.3.

Like buttons, plastic press studs can be transparent or colour matched to materials and often the visible face of metal or plastic studs carries the logo or decal of the producer.

Rivets

Whilst these are not closure parts, they are widely used for decorative and reinforcement purposes on denim garments. Rivets require an appropriate device to set them on garments.

Zips

Although slide fasteners, as they were then called, were introduced in 1912, it took about another 20 years before they started to be used for men's and women's clothing. Since then zips (Figure 4.4) have become one of the most extensively used closure methods utilised by the clothing industry. Apart from their functional purposes, zips are also used for decorative effects or as design features. Zips are a continuous form of closure as against buttons which are intermittent.

Construction

Tape – The majority of zip tapes are twill woven from 100% polyester, which produces a strong, light weight tape that does not shrink. Knitted zip tapes are soft and pliable and are mostly used for garments made from knitted fabrics.

Chain – This element is also referred to as the teeth or scoops and they are made from metal or plastic materials. Metal scoops are stamped out of brass or aluminium and are then clamped on to the beaded edge of the tape. Alternatively, continuous monofilament coils made from nylon or polyester are woven directly into the tape edge. Zips with coiled chains are lighter and more flexible than those with metal chains.

Slider – The function of the slider is to engage or disengage the opposite sides of the chain as it is moved up or down. The slider can be non-locking or can have a built-in or semi or fully automatic locking action. An automatic locking slider is very dependable although it is bulkier than the other two types.

Top and bottom stops – These prevent the loss of the slider caused through excessive up or down movement. For zips whose top ends are caught in the waist band seaming, the top stops are often dispensed with as the stitching serves as stops. The bottom stop prevents the zip from being opened to the lower end of the tape and thus jamming the slider.

Pull tab – This enables the consumer to easily move the slider in the desired direction. Tabs are produced in a great variety of shapes and finishes and are frequently used for decorative purposes.

Zip Types

There are several types of zips available, which enables the designer to select a zip that is the most suitable for a particular garment or end use. Some of the more commonly used zips are given here.

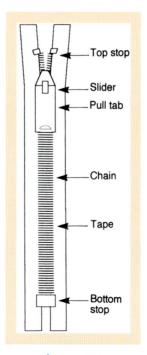

Figure 4.4.

Standard type – Used in different lengths for skirts, dresses and other articles of clothing. This zip is usually inserted into a seam and whilst the zip is concealed, the setting stitching shows on the outside of the garment. To set this type of zip, a half presser foot is used which enables the operator to sew close to the chain.

Invisible zip – So called because the zip and its setting stitching cannot be seen on the right side of the opening. The insertion of this zip requires a special type of presser foot and the setting operation itself is shorter and easier than for a standard zip.

Separated zip – This type of zip is utilised when the garment can be worn either closed or fully opened. Some typical applications of open-ended zips are for blousons, parka jackets and zip-out linings.

Continuous zip – Used for men's trousers and all categories of jeans, continuous zips with an average length of 50 m are wound onto reels with the metal chain closed or separated into left and right sides. This permits each side of the zip to be set onto the respective panels before the crotch seam is closed. The slider and bottom stop are fitted by means of small mechanical devices located in suitable positions along the production line.

Continuous metal zips are cheaper in use than those made to specific lengths as they can be cut to the exact lengths required and there is no need to maintain regular stocks of different lengths or the odds and ends which are bound to accumulate.

Hook and Loop Fastening (Velcro)

These are pressure sensitive tapes, which have gained widespread acceptance as a closure method for many sportswear articles and items of children's clothing. They consist of two nylon pile tapes, one having a surface of loops and the other a surface of microscopic hooks. When the two pile surfaces are pressed together, the hooks engage the loops creating a closure area the size of the tape. The closure is opened by pulling the two tapes apart.

Pressure sensitive tapes are far more visible and are bulkier than buttons or zips but are simpler to use, especially for cold sportsmen and women or small children. It is not advisable to use these tapes on knitted or looped materials because the strong nylon hooks are liable to damage the fabric.

Shoulder Pads

Padding in various forms and on different locations of the body has been used for clothing for about three thousand years, and during the past hundred years or so pads have become a standard shaping medium for the shoulder line. Today, shoulder pads are very much a styling and fashion factor and the designer frequently has to select new shapes and thicknesses.

Pads can be made from foam or layers of non-woven materials built up around a central foam or fibre layer. For unlined garments a pad covered with polyamide or self-material is generally used, and for lined garments there is no necessity to cover the pad. There are pads specifically for washable garments and for garments which are to be dry cleaned only. Care should be taken that the pad selected matches up with the cleaning conditions on the care label of the garment. The pads for unlined garments can be attached by a series of tacks made by a button sewing machine or what is called a blindstitch tacker. For tailored garments, the pads can be sewn in or fused to the shoulder area with small areas of thermoplastic resin positioned on the top layer of the pad.

Tapes

These are narrow bands of woven fabric which are used for the following purposes in the make up of clothing:

Decorative – for binding the edges of collars, lapels and flaps, etc.
Stretch control – to prevent seams or edges from stretching during making up.
Finishing – sometimes used instead of overlocking on visible seam and hem edges.

Bought-in tapes can be straight or on the bias, depending on their end use, and are available in a large range of widths, colours and finishes. Examples of their use are:

Decorative

These can be sewn to edges with or without turning in the edges of the tape itself. Figure 4.5A shows the application of a flat tape and Figure 4.5B the formation of a double turned tape.

Stretch control (Figure 4.6) – a narrow straight pre-positioned tape is used for this purpose and it is caught into the stitching when the seam or edge is sewn. Armholes, shoulders and sewn fitted waistlines are often taped in this fashion.

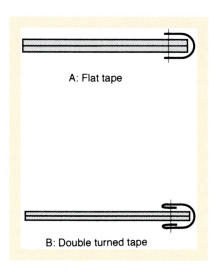

A: Flat tape

B: Double turned tape

Figure 4.5A & B.

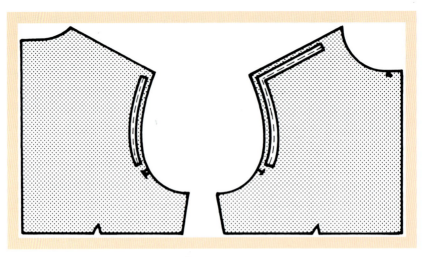

Figure 4.6.

Finishing

Bias tapes, cut from the same lining as used for the half-lining of the garment, are used to neaten and finish the edges of the visible seams and hem. This method is sometimes used to enclose raw edges instead of overlocking.

The application of tapes requires special folders and/or guides and prefer-ably a mechanical device which controls the tension and feed of the tape whilst it is being sewn to the garment. Binding the collar and lapels of a garment is a highly skilled and lengthy operation mostly due to the necessity to clean-finish the corners of the lapels and collars. Designers should carefully consider including this type of garment in a collection because they are not very welcome products in the majority of factories.

CHAPTER 5

Designing for Manufacture

Some of the processes of design have been described in earlier chapters. However, the relationships between designers and production technologists have their own complexities. A designer is the one with the flair to innovate and create new product designs; the production technologist has to interpret the designs and maintain the design integrity whilst being a realist in developing the design into mass production. It is sometimes here where problems and conflict arise and must be appropriately managed.

The success of any product is dependent upon a number of factors that are ultimately linked together through a series of processes and activities. These components can decide the outcome of whether the product will sell to the consumer. As customers have become more discerning, manufacturers have had to come up with new and innovative ways of persuading customers to buy their products. In addition to this, global competition in the clothing sector has added an extra dimension of pressure on individual clothing manufacturers to maintain their already decreasing market share.

In manufacturing, there are a number of internal and external factors that need to be taken into account before, during and after manufacture. This constitutes a multi-disciplinary team working approach from all concerned at the start of the design process and during the production chain. This is in contrast to usual practices, namely a step by step approach which is practised by most manufacturing companies and in which the design is passed to the process planning, to manufacturing and then to sales in a sequential manner. The alternative method is to design the product to be compatible with the existing manufacturing system. This simultaneous approach would seem to make sense when considering it has been estimated that between 70% and 80% of final production costs might be determined by design.

PROCESS BEGINS WITH DESIGN

Ultimately, the process of production begins on the catwalk, at street level style or in the content of fashion media and this is where the high street and department stores get their ideas, based upon the innovative creations from the named and popular designers. The concept of creative design manifests itself in many different ways that may include expanding and challenging boundaries, breaking taboos and ultimately altering the concept of design that people may have created in their own mind. Many of these designs eventually spill over into the general market from the major clothing retailers anxious to be the first to exploit the new creations.

It is generally the case that the design of the product has been completed before manufacturing is considered. This methodology could be held responsible for many of the crisis management problems that prevail within the manufacturing system. The first rule of commercial design has been broken: namely, does the company have the resources and expertise to manufacture this product in quantity? In the majority of these cases, the answer is neither *yes* nor *no* but we have to manufacture it anyway. If this problem ever arises, then the communication process has completely disintegrated which could significantly increase the costs to the business, as well as the stress levels for all concerned.

The formation of multi-disciplinary teams is an important factor in improving communication skills and addressing various concepts simultaneously, which can lead to an integrated and balanced situation between the design and manufacturing process.

The positive elements are that coordination between members of all departments will be significantly improved. In addition, decisions affecting the success of a product are emphasised as being the main objective rather than the individual interest of each department.

DESIGNING FOR PRODUCE-ABILITY

Once the customer has accepted the design, there is very little that can be done about it except to make the product. It is at this stage that attempts to introduce value engineering usually take place (Figure 5.1). This type of technique concentrates on reducing the cost of manufacture after the design has been completed. The problem faced by the manufacturing department is being able to make sufficient quantity in order for the product to be profitable. Therefore, value engineering becomes an integral part of the manufacturing process.

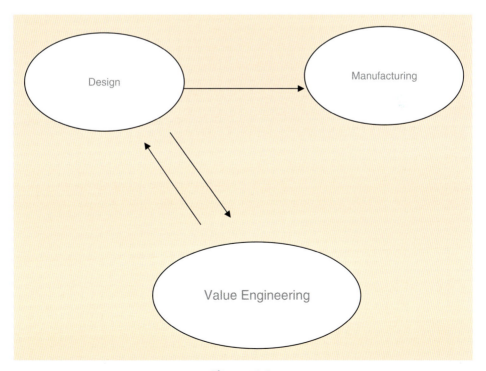

Figure 5.1.

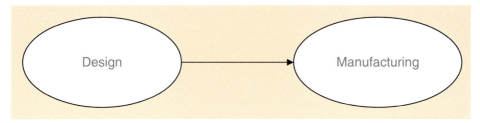

Figure 5.2.

With large manufacturing companies, the concept of value engineering is easier to implement because a greater amount of resources can be utilised to combat any specific problems that might arise or have arisen. With smaller companies however, this is not the case and therefore the company may have to rely on their wits in order to enact a solution.

Many companies do not implement such a system and proceed from the design process directly to manufacturing (Figure 5.2). This may be because the pay-off of preventing problems during the development stages is difficult to quantify. However, though the amounts in figures may be debatable, there is no doubt that it makes logical sense to solve the problems at the design stage rather than in the manufacturing area. At this stage, it is very unlikely that anything can be done to rectify the situation and serious problems in manufacture could ensue. Fire fighting is best left alone to those with the expertise and ability. It should have no place in a production environment. Effective communications between the design and production teams could mean that the manufacture of a product could be considered as soon as the design commences. This will also have the added advantage that it gives product engineers a sense of ownership in the product.

HARMONIOUS INTERACTION

It is vital that senior management are seen to create the environment in which teams of people can work together. Japanese companies have been using this methodology for so long that its people cannot remember working in any other way. Their methods of working have been integrated into this country very successfully since the latter quarter of the 20th century, particularly within the motor industry. This methodology is still not apparent within the textile industry however. A team working approach has to be created and then nurtured in order for it to bear the fruits of success. This means taking a long term strategic view rather than a short term approach (Figure 5.3). Team members are best left alone to their own resources in order for them to function effectively. They need to have autonomy and control over their own environment which is a factor that traditional management have not been in favour of, as they see an eroding of their own power base. Unfortunately, because of this mindset, the most essential element of any working environment is overlooked, namely that of

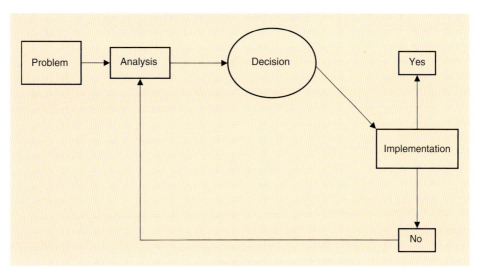

Figure 5.3.

getting the job done. Interaction amongst human beings, if channelled correctly, provides the ultimate solution to problem solving (Figure 5.4). Therefore, careful planning and preparation can harmonise most of the problems related at the design stage and integration into the production chain can be implemented very successfully.

Figure 5.4.

FIRE FIGHTING VERSUS PRECLUSION

Fire fighting is a destructive force, which can start with a spark and quickly develop into an inferno. Once the spark has become an inferno, the means of control has become very difficult. Therefore, the old adage that has been chronicled on many occasions that prevention is the best form of cure would seem to be the best policy. However, this analogy is tainted by the fact that due to pressures imparted on individuals to produce ever increasing quantities of product, decision making is often made on the hoof. This reduces the power of the thought process and often leads to a bad or ill thought out decision. The power of thinking can be a formidable tool if it is used wisely but many people cannot identify the ways in which they think and how these processes link up with the thought content. Thinking skills enable anyone to access the hidden mental pictures that underlie action, which are vital aspects of implementation from the design stage to the finished product. Manufacturing problems should be precluded in the design process through the application of these skills.

PART 2

GARMENT TECHNOLOGY

CHAPTER 6

Understanding Textile Materials

Designers need to have a good degree of knowledge of textile materials, their performance and properties.

Textiles and clothing have been synonymous with human activity for thousands of years and as the years have progressed, the usage has become wider and more varied. The wearing of clothing for example, has become more diverse as new fabrics have been developed. Generations of fashion gurus have emerged anxious to exploit the market with new and innovative creations.

Where fashion and aesthetics are concerned, one of the crucial aspects of manufacturing apparel is how the garment looks and handles when it has been made. Prehistoric men and women used animal skins and plants to protect them from the cold and against the sun, sand and dust. This can be described as the birth of textiles and became the start of the revolution that has become a multibillion-pound global industry.

NATURAL FIBRES

From those early days of plants and animal skins, fibres were extracted and other natural fibres followed so that now we exploit four main sources of natural materials, which are:

- Bast fibre such as flax, jute, ramie, hemp.
- Wool and other animal hairs.
- Cotton.
- Silk.

Only the most common natural fibres used in the manufacture of apparel are discussed here.

Cellulose Fibres

The cellulose fibres are the fibres that are produced naturally from plants. The most important of these fibres, cotton (Figures 6.1 and 6.2), is the most widely used in the world and accounts for over 50% of the world's production. It is used extensively in apparel, home-ware and outerwear, and is recognised for its comfort and breathability and also for its ability to absorb moisture; thus making it comfortable against the skin. It is blended extensively with polyester and is used in many applications particularly in the manufacture of shirting. The crease resistance properties of the polyester combined with the comfort and moisture regain of cotton produce the label on the shirt of "easy care", the most common blend ratio being 65% polyester and 35% cotton. This makes the ironing of this type of garment much easier.

Under a microscope, the cotton fibre appears as a very fine regular fibre and can range in length from 10 mm to 65 mm depending upon the quality of the fibre. The longer the fibre is, the better quality yarn can be spun resulting in a more comfortable and better quality product.

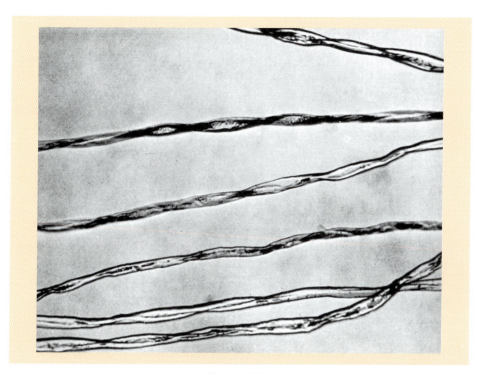

Figure 6.1.

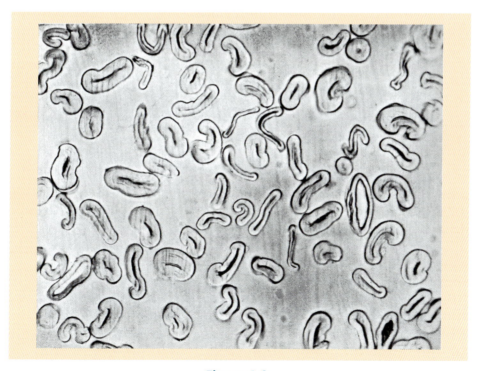

Figure 6.2.

Other properties of cotton are:

- It is one of the only fibres that gets stronger when it is wet enabling a smoother manufacturing process when weaving into fabric due to being able to withstand the rigours of the weaving process.
- It is a relatively strong fibre due to its polymer structure and its crystalline nature.
- It is relatively inelastic due to its crystalline nature.
- Cotton is a hydrophilic fibre due to its amorphous regions making it able to absorb up to 50% moisture when wet.
- It has the ability to conduct heat energy minimising any destructive heat accumulation and thus can withstand very hot ironing temperatures.
- Cotton fibres are weakened and destroyed by acids.

Dyes for Dyeing Cotton

The dyestuffs used to dye cotton vary in their application and quality, the cheapest of these generally being direct dyes. These dyes have only moderate light fastness and also some have moderate to poor wash fastness so care must be taken to avoid washing bright colours with white materials for example

Reactive dyes are used extensively and are generally better quality. These have much better quality in having a much higher light fastness and wash fastness and are very resistant to the degrading effects of ultraviolet light, radiation of sunlight and air pollutants.

Sulphur dyes have good wash fastness properties but only a fair light fastness. This is attributed to the lack of resistance by the sulphur dye molecules to the photochemical effects of the sunlight ultraviolet radiation.

Vat dyes are the highest quality of all the dyes for dying cotton. Often shirts will have the name vat dyed on the label. They have excellent light fastness and wash fastness and have excellent resistance against the degrading effects of ultraviolet degradation of sunlight and air pollutants. There are some exceptions to this however, an example being indigo.

Flax

Another fibre commonly used in the production of apparel is flax (Figures 6.3 and 6.4) normally known as linen. Linen is the term applied to yarn spun from the flax fibres. It is a heavier fibre than cotton and it is for this reason that most linen materials are of light construction. Heavier linen materials would be uncomfortably heavy to wear.

The fibre morphology (appearance) of linen is that of a much thicker fibre than cotton and much longer, ranging in length from 10 cm to 100 cm. The colour of flax varies from light blond to grey blond, and the differences in shade results from the agricultural and climatic conditions in which it was grown.

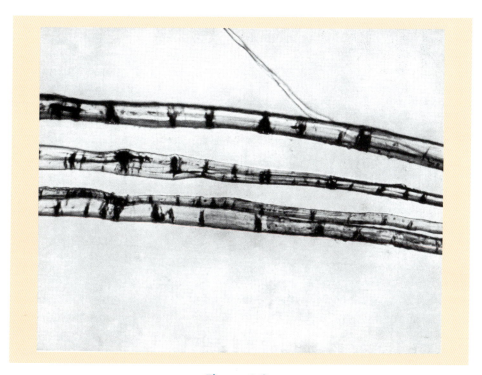

Figure 6.3.

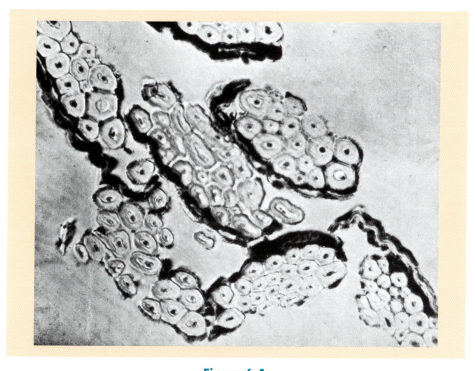

Figure 6.4.

Other properties of flax are:

- It is a very strong fibre due to its high crystalline nature.
- It is very inelastic, again due to its polymer structure and crystalline nature.
- Flax is a hydrophilic fibre due to its amorphous regions making it able to absorb up to 50% moisture when wet.
- The explanations of acids for cotton also apply to flax.
- The same dyestuffs used in the dyeing of cotton are also used for dyeing flax.

Protein Fibres

Protein fibres are the resultant product from an animal and these include wool, silk, mohair, alpaca, angora, cashmere, etc. Only the most commonly used protein fibres, namely wool and silk, are considered here.

Wool (Figures 6.5 and 6.6) is the fibre from fleece of domesticated sheep. It is a natural, protein and multi-cellular staple fibre. It is a crimped fine to thick regular fibre that has natural serrations (scales) along its length. This fibre has a very high natural crease resistance and very good resilience partly attributable to the elastic nature of the wool fibre. The warmth of wool fabrics is due more to the air spaces in the material than to the fibres.

Other properties of wool are:

- It is a relatively weak fibre with a low tensile strength.
- Wool has a very high absorbency of approximately 100%.

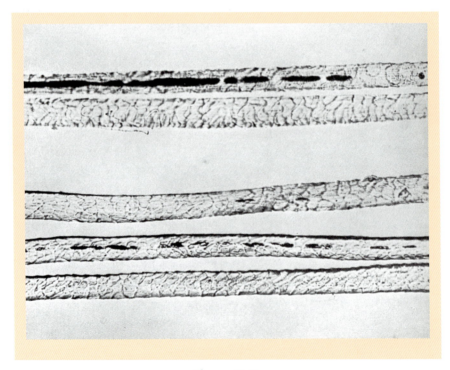

Figure 6.5.

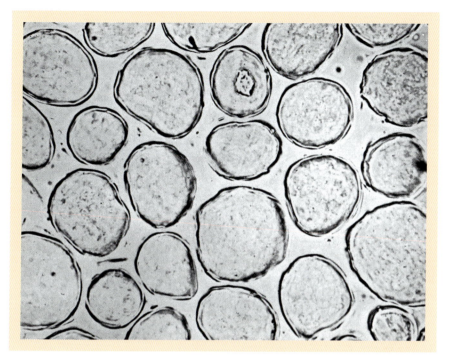

Figure 6.6.

- Wool has very good elastic recovery and excellent resilience due to its crimped configuration.
- Wool is more resistant to acids than to alkalis.
- Exposure to sunlight and weather tends to yellow or dull coloured wool textile materials.

Dyes for Dyeing Wool

Wool like cotton is considered to be a relatively easy fibre to dye. The dyes most effective for dyeing wool are acid dyes, chrome or mordant dyes, premetallised dyes and reactive dyes. Like all natural fibres, the dye molecules can only enter the amorphous regions of the polymer system, amorphous being the areas within the fibre where the dye can be absorbed in terms of moisture.

Silk Fibres

Silk (Figures 6.7 and 6.8) is a very fine fibre with translucent filaments and is used extensively in the silk manufacture of apparel particularly shirts, dresses and ties. The raw silk strands are encased by a protein called sericin which enables the fibre to withstand prolonged exposure to weather making the fibre weather resistant due to this coating of sericin.

The silk filament has a high degree of strength associated with it but when the fibre gets wet it loses strength and the fibre is more sensitive to heat than wool

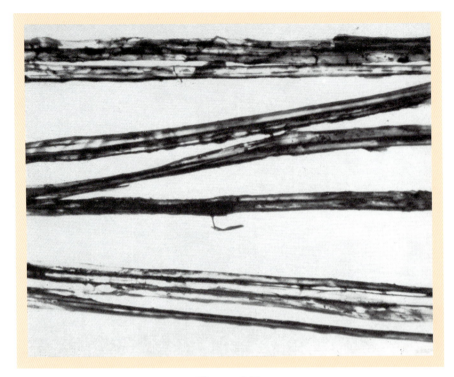

Figure 6.7.

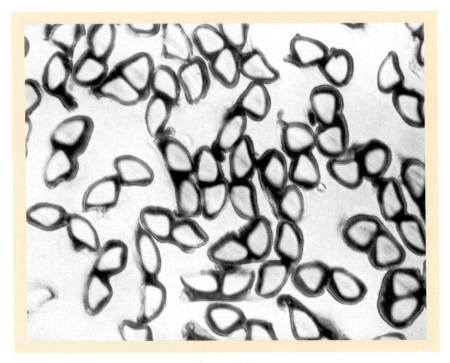

Figure 6.8.

due to chemical interactions within the fibre. The fibre is more degraded by acids than wool and the resistance to the environment is not as good.

The explanations and descriptions of the dyeing of wool also apply to silk, but with silk being a more lustrous fibre than wool, the dyed and printed textile materials made from silk will appear to be much brighter.

SYNTHETIC FIBRES

Because of the many and diverse numbers of synthetic fibres, only two of the most common ones used extensively for apparel manufacturing are briefly considered here. Synthetic fibres are manmade fibres made from materials such as coal and other substances and chemicals. The most common of the fibres used are acrylics, polyester and viscose.

Viscose

Viscose (Figures 6.9 and 6.10) is a manmade fibre made from natural fibre materials such as tree bark. It is usually described as a regenerated cellulose fibre. The morphology of the fibre is as follows:

- It is a fine regular filament or staple fibre.
- Its cross section is that of a kidney bean shape.

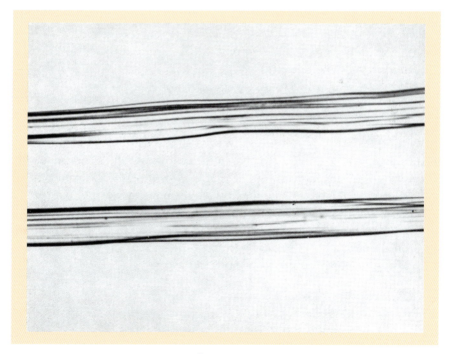

Figure 6.9.

Figure 6.10.

- It has a harsh bright lustrous appearance.
- It is treated with chemicals to make the fibre appear to be white.
- It is very amorphous meaning it absorbs water very easily.
- It is a weaker fibre than cotton.
- When wet viscose is only half its strength when it is dry.

Polyester

Polyester (Figures 6.11 and 6.12) is the most common of all the manmade fibres. It is considered to be a rather heavy fibre and for this reason is manufactured as light weight or thin fabrics since thick polyester materials would be too heavy. This fibre is used extensively in the production of apparel, blended with cotton to manufacture shirts, blouses, underwear and suiting fabrics, trousers and many other products such as high performance outwear jackets, ski wear, tents and car seat covers. Some of the properties of polyester are:

- It is a fine, regular and translucent fibre.
- It is hydrophobic (highly resistant to water penetration).
- It can be crimped and textured.

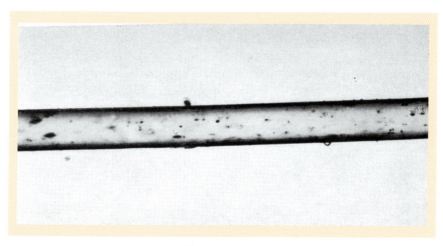

Figure 6.11.

- It has good easy care properties especially when blended with cotton.
- It is highly crystalline making it water resistant.
- It has high tenacity (strength).
- It has very good colour fastness.

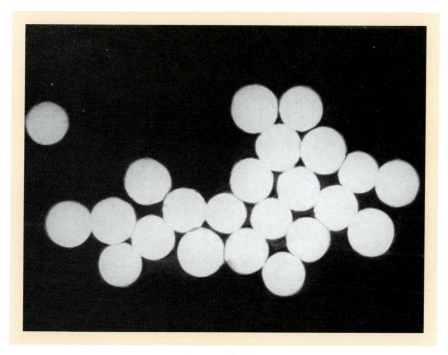

Figure 6.12.

Dyes for Dyeing Polyester

It is a difficult fibre to dye. The dyes used for dyeing polyester were developed specifically for this fibre and are called disperse dyes. The fibre/fabric needs to be heated to quite a high temperature in order for the dye to enter the fibre polymer system.

THE PRINCIPLES OF WEAVING

The definition of weaving is the interlacing of the warp and weft yarns to create cloth. Weaving derived from basket making and it is the earliest form of fabric manufacture going back to 7000 BC. By the end of the Roman period weaving was a highly developed form of technology. The earliest fabrics were made exclusively from plant fibre and protein fibres such as wool were not developed until around 2500 BC and silk from around 1500 BC.

These first-generation textiles were colourless and were used principally for protection against the environment. The next revolutionary step was the creation of the knowledge to colour these fibres and fabrics. Initially these garments were expensive and only the very rich could afford them. The representation of an image became important and this became the start of the fashion explosion. Today fashion is available at very reasonable prices. Figures 6.13 and 6.14 present fashion from the 1950's to the present day.

Figure 6.13.

Figure 6.14.

Woven Fabric Designs

There are hundreds of different fabric constructions, the most common being plain-woven fabrics, to more complex structures such as twill, herringbone, satin and sateen weaves.

Fabrics are designed on point paper similar to graph paper. The design method is given as:

- Pattern draft of point paper design.
- It is marked and read from bottom left to top right.
- The vertical columns represent the warp yarns and the horizontal rows represent the weft yarns.
- A mark placed over any weft cell indicates that the warp is lifted over the weft in that intersection.
- An absence of a mark indicates the opposite, i.e. warp remains beneath the weft yarn.

An example of a point paper design for a plain-woven fabric is given in Figure 6.15 and an example of the fabric is given in Figure 6.16 and Figure 6.17.

Properties of a plain-woven fabric are:

- The fabric is the simplest and tightest of interlacing warp and weft yarns.
- Opposite sides of the fabrics are the same.

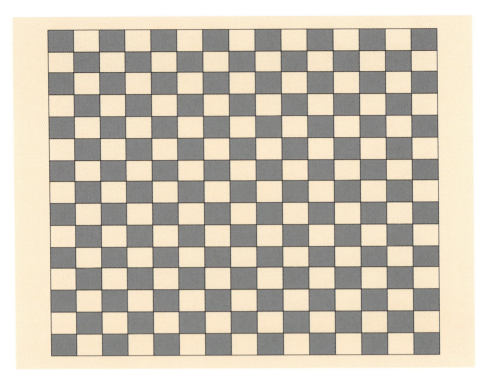

Figure 6.15.

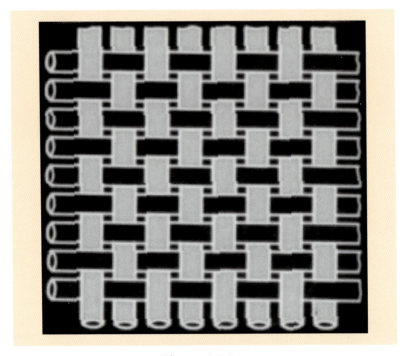

Figure 6.16.

Figure 6.17.

- These fabrics have high abrasion and are resistant to yarn slippage.
- Types of fabrics produced include batiste, cambric, Donegal, fresco and voile.

Twill Weaves

A twill weave (Figures 6.18–6.21B) is a fabric composed of yarns in a diagonal line where each warp yarn lifts over (and/or remains over) more than one weft.
    Properties of the twill fabric are:

- The twill fabric order of interlacing causes diagonal lines to appear in the fabric.
- These lines can either run in the Z direction or the S direction.
- Warp faced twills show a predominance of warp yarns on the face of the fabric.
- Weft faced twills show a predominance of weft yarns on the face of the fabric.

Satin and Sateen Fabrics

Satin and sateen (Figures 6.22A–6.23B) fabrics use a high density of warp and weft faced yarns to produce materials. They are smooth, uniform and lustrous due to the scarcity of interlacings and the density of threads.
    Examples of these fabrics are given below:

Figure 6.18.

Figure 6.19.

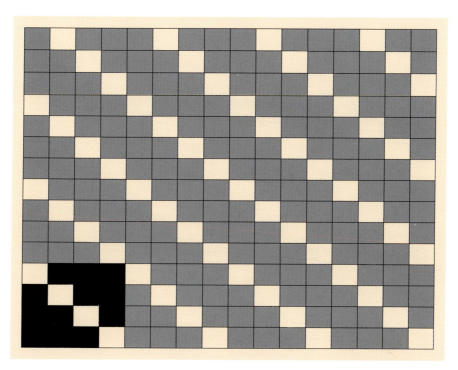

Figure 6.20A.

Figure 6.20B.

Figure 6.21A.

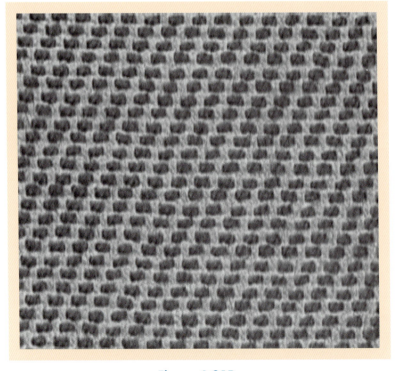

Figure 6.21B.

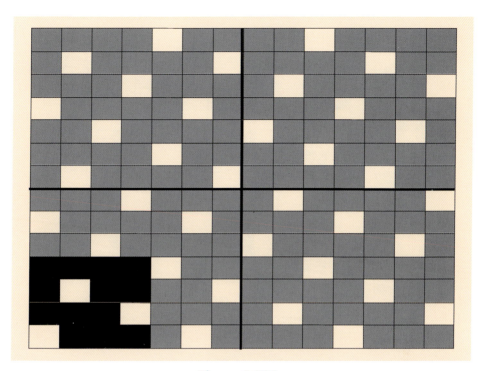

Figure 6.22A.

Figure 6.22B.

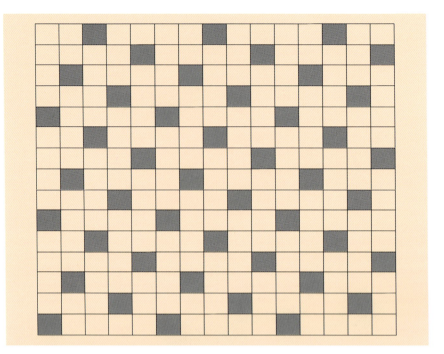

Figure 6.23A.

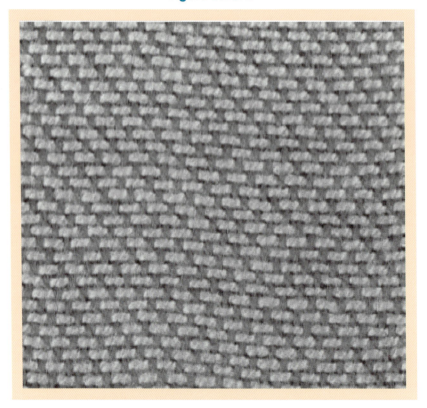

Figure 6.23B.

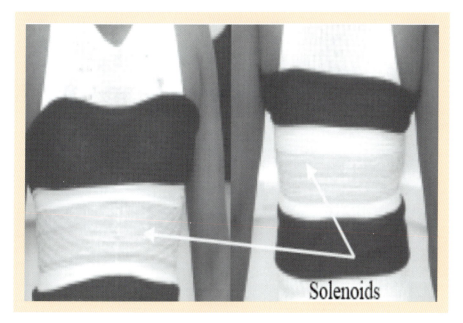
Solenoids

Figure 6.24.

FUTURE TEXTILES FOR FASHION

The change in the functionality of textiles has evolved from the first generation of textile materials, from those that provide a barrier to the elements to the evolution of the second generation, providing a barrier and projecting an image.

The previous generations of fabrics can be described as passive, not able to adapt to environmental changes. However, materials are being developed that are able to adapt to the environment where fibres, yarns and fabrics are being combined with electronics to produce smart materials – a third generation of textile materials. These electronic components include:

- Strain gauges.
- Flexible switches.
- Displacement transducers.
- Electrodes.
- Temperature transducers.

These produce electrically active fibre structures with significant electrical properties in order to incorporate conductive elements into the fabric structure.

Garments have been designed and developed to measure respiratory movements (Figure 6.24), heart beat and blood pressure. Work is being done to design garments that that can incorporate the SIM from a mobile phone so you can have a telephone call without having to use a handset.

CHAPTER 7

Sample Cutting

PREPARATION FOR CUTTING

Introduction

For all practical purposes the sample room is the research and development department of a clothing factory, and one of the technical aspects which have to be examined is cutting. Before a sample garment can be mass produced its practicability and efficiency as regards cutting have to be ensured; it is irresponsible and costly to present the cutting room with unresolved problems. It is worth bearing in mind that if something does not work in the sample room, it certainly will not work in the cutting room.

Garment Pattern and Fabric

There are four elements that have to be considered before starting to cut samples:

(1) The pattern: as a medium of communication and as a production tool
(2) Grain lines: establishing the linear relationship between the garment pattern and the cloth
(3) Pile direction: how this influences pattern component arrangements
(4) Fabric pattern: what has to be taken into account.

The sample garment may be cut out by the pattern cutter; however, that part of the process may be passed on to another member of the team to complete.

(1) The Pattern

The initial sample is cut from the designer pattern. This may consist of the larger pattern pieces as half patterns, which have to be cut to the fold of fabric. In addition one pattern piece for paired sections of the garment will usually suffice as long as the instructions show how many pieces are to be cut. All the pattern pieces should be fully annotated, notched and contain grain lines. When the garment is approved for production the patterns used should contain full pattern pieces.

The production pattern is the primary link between design and production and so must communicate accurately with all the functions that have to use the pattern. These functions are pattern grading, marker planning and sewing, and the pattern has to clearly and precisely convey the information necessary to perform each of these operations. This information is conveyed by numbers, marks and notches, etc., and not by separate written instructions. New sample patterns always require some explanation, but there should be no necessity for verbal or written working instructions when it comes to production. The pattern should tell the complete story to all concerned.

In the case of the production pattern, there should be a pattern piece for every component to be cut. Marker planners or cutters are not expected to be pattern makers or pattern guessers, therefore pattern sets must be complete in every respect. Each pattern part must be marked with grain lines and direction indicators. Patterns should be paired when the garment is to be cut from open rather than folded fabric. Two practical methods of pairing patterns are by marks and by colour:

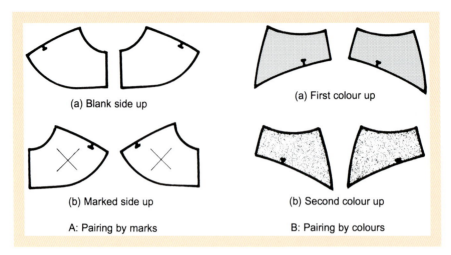

(a) Blank side up

(a) First colour up

(b) Marked side up

(b) Second colour up

A: Pairing by marks

B: Pairing by colours

Figure 7.1A & B.

- By marks (Figure 7.1A) – Cut pairs for each component and mark an X on one side only of each of the two components when they are in a paired position. The blank sides indicate correct pairing, as do the marked sides.
- By colour (Figure 7.1B) – This method requires a pattern card with a different colour on each side. Staple two pieces of the card together with the same colour inside, and then cut out the components. Pairing is achieved when the same colour shows for a pair of the same component.

Patterns for asymmetrical garments should be prepared for positioning on the right side of the cloth only. A simple method to ensure the correct face-up positioning is to mark the reverse side of the fabric components with a large X.

Every pattern piece must be clearly identified as regards style number, garment type and size, the fabric for which the pattern is intended and the number of components in a set for a particular material, i.e. cloth, lining and interlinings. Pattern identification (Figure 7.2) is very important be it on a physical or digital incarnation of the pattern.

Brand Fashions	
Style number	6114
Comp. number	HC 20 664
Garment type	Straight Coat
Size	42
Material	Lining
# Pieces	6
Component	back

Figure 7.2.

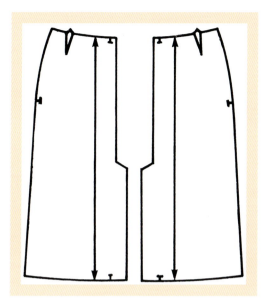

Figure 7.3.

(2) Grain Lines

This refers to the positioning of pattern components in relation to the true length of the fabric. For woven materials this line is the warp threads and for knitted fabrics it is the wales.

A garment will hang in a direct relationship to the grain directions of the body components. If the grain lines are incorrect, the finished garment will have a distorted appearance which cannot be rectified. This also applies to sleeves which are sewn to the body, such as set-in, raglan and dolman. In many instances wavy hemlines are also a direct result of off-grain components. Therefore it is essential that each pattern component is marked with a grain line on both sides for its complete length (Figure 7.3). The grain line is also often used as a datum line when digitising patterns for computerised grading.

As a general guide, the grain lines for main components are:

- Fronts – Parallel to the centre front.
- Backs – Parallel to the centre back.
- Sleeves – On or parallel to the true centre line.
- Lapel facings – The grain line runs parallel to the edge of the lapel section. If this positioning produces an acute bias angle on the lower part of the facing, it is sometimes permitted to make a join across the facing between the top and second buttonhole.
- Patch pockets – Relative to their position on the front, the grain line is parallel to that of the front.
- Inset pockets – For piped, welted and similar types of inset pockets, the grain line runs along the length of the pocket piece or pieces.

- Top collars – On the centre back line of the collar.
- Under collars – These can be omnidirectional because the grain line of the inter-lining used for this component is the controlling grain line. It serves no practical purpose in mass production to insist that under collars are cut on the true bias whilst top collars are cut according to the straight grain.

- Other parts – Generally, the grain lines can be derived from the grain line of the component on which the part is located.

Some typical examples of grain line markings are shown in Figure 7.4.

Whilst there are firm principles involved in the determination of grain lines, sometimes design features and practical considerations have to be given prefer-ence, especially with checked fabrics. For example, matching a patch pocket on a check material demands a considerable amount of work in cutting and sewing. The designer could consider cutting the pocket on the true bias which would greatly reduce the difficulties of this operation. It is sometimes necessary to make practical compromises and the designer has to be prepared to weigh up the pros and cons of alternative courses of action. A little common sense goes a long way, especially when labour costs are concerned.

(3) Pile Direction

This describes the lay (direction), length and density of the protruding fibres on the surface of the right side of the cloth. The question regarding pile is to what

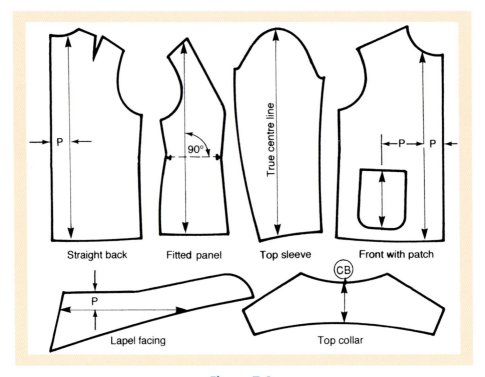

Figure 7.4.

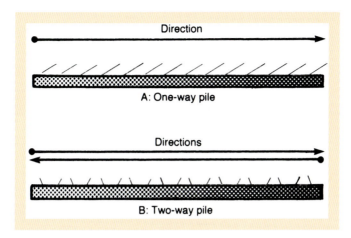

Figure 7.5A & B.

extent it influences the positioning of pattern components on the cloth whilst observing the grain line markings. All fabrics have a pile factor and for practical purposes they can be grouped under three headings:

(1) One-way (Figure 7.5A) – On these fabrics there is a prominent pile which lays in one direction only. Typical examples of this type of cloth are corduroy, velvet and mohair. Due to the very definite pile lay, the components of all the sizes in a cutting marker must be positioned in one direction only.

(2) Two-way (Figure 7.5B) – This type of cloth is one of the most widely used in the clothing industry because the pile factor allows for higher utilisation than with one-way fabrics. Whilst these cloths do have a pile factor it is minimal, and this permits the positioning of components for each size in opposite directions. This method of positioning patterns in a cutting marker is often referred to as "one-up, one-down". Figure 7.6 shows two markers planned according to different pile conditions.

(3) No-pile – Although this heading is a misnomer, it refers to materials which have a virtually negligible pile factor. This enables components for one size to be positioned in opposite directions. Caution is however necessary as some fabric can appear shaded if cut in opposite directions of the fabric.

Preparing the Pattern

To ensure the correct positioning of the garment pattern within the cutting marker, every component has to be marked on both sides with direction indicators. Under most circumstances these indicators can be marked on the grain line and Figure 7.7 shows the application of this method for the alternative positioning procedures. It is worth bearing in mind that garment patterns are not always used for one fabric exclusively, so every new fabric which is to be cut from a previously used production pattern must be checked for its pile factor and the pattern markings changed if necessary.

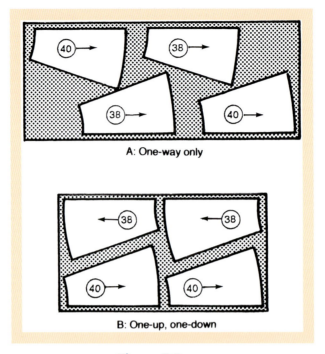

A: One-way only

B: One-up, one-down

Figure 7.6.

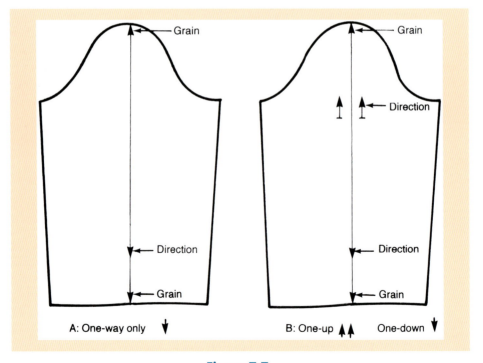

A: One-way only

B: One-up

One-down

Figure 7.7.

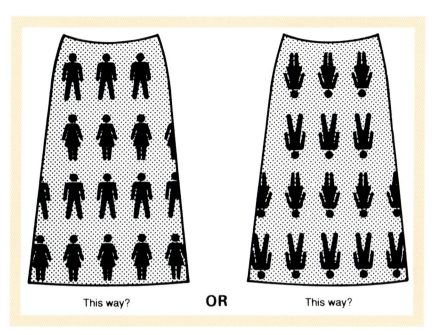

This way?   **OR**   This way?

Figure 7.8.

(4) Fabric Pattern

This refers to the form of the pattern on the right side of the cloth, and has three aspects:

(1) One-way (Figure 7.8) – This is where the pattern form dictates that the garment patterns for every size in the cutting marker must be positioned in one direction only. For example, if the motif on a printed fabric is an upright human figure then it is preferable that the figures stand on their feet and not on their heads.

(2) Two-way (Figure 7.9) – This type of pattern form has a definite direction but it is not sufficiently dominant to warrant one-way only positioning. In most cases the pattern components for each size can be positioned one-up, one-down, but this decision has to be carefully evaluated.

Consider the situation in a retail shop where two garments of the same style and fabric, but cut in opposite directions, are hanging side by side on a display rail. Would the difference in cloth pattern direction be easily noticeable or would it be sufficiently "blurred" to be of little consequence? There are no rules for this subject, which means that a large element of objective judgement is called for.

(3) Non-directional (Figure 7.10) – This type of pattern form has no definite directions and, subject to the pile factor, pattern components for one size can be positioned in either length direction.

Patterned fabrics also include checks and stripes and these will be examined in the final section of this chapter.

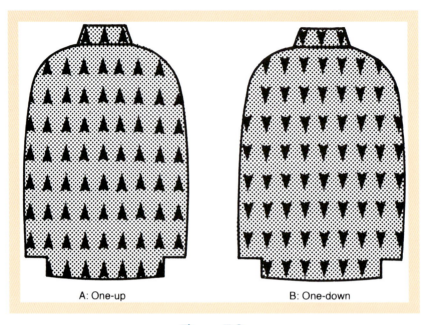

Figure 7.9.

MARKER PLANNING

Introduction

To cut a sample garment, the pattern components have to be economically arranged according to their grain lines and the pile direction of the fabric which is to be cut. The regular form of this arrangement is a rectangle with the short

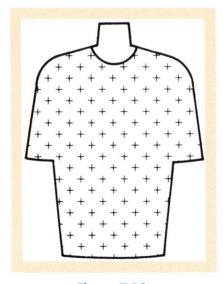

Figure 7.10.

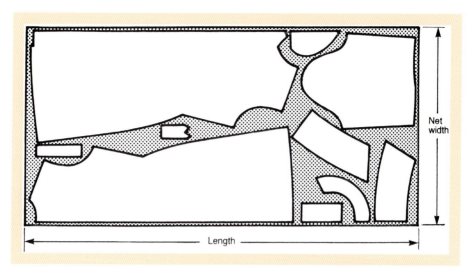

Net width

Length

Figure 7.11.

side equivalent to the net width of the fabric and the long side the length required to contain the pattern components. The drawing of this arrangement is a cutting marker (Figure 7.11) and when starting to prepare markers, there are a number of procedures which have to be followed. This starts by determining the net width of the cloth to be cut, which can be easily done but there are some practical considerations involved.

Net Width

This is sometimes called the "cutable" width and both terms refer to the width remaining after the measurements of the two selvedges have been deducted from the gross width of the fabric. With most woven materials the selvedges are constructed from stronger warp threads than those used for the fabric itself. As the selvedge is stronger it is also thicker and very likely to have a different shrinkage factor from that of the fabric. It is not advisable to include this type of selvedge in garments.

The selvedges of many light weight woven materials are constructed from the same warp threads as the fabric, and this enables the selvedge to be utilised if needed. Often the selvedge is used for the inside edge of facings on shirts and blouses, which is a saving in cutting and overlocking.

Most knitted fabrics are produced in tubular form and are then slit open in their length. As the slitting process is not always 100% accurate, some allowance has to be made for possible irregularities in the width. In addition, the edges could have slight damages caused by the pin-plates or clips which hold the fabric in position when it is being fed through a stentering machine to stabilise the finished width of the fabric.

Flat-knit fabrics have finished edges, but they also go through the stentering process, which could leave small damages along the edges. The practical conclusion is that the edges of all open knitted fabrics should be carefully examined in order to determine the correct net width of the fabric.

Principles of Marker Planning
Manual Planning

There are no fixed rules for the manual planning of cutting markers because in the main this process relies on the perceptual sense of the planner and the ability to "see" the best interlocking combination of the pattern components. Nevertheless, there are a number of principles which can be applied.

Before starting to plan the marker there are some preparatory procedures to perform:

- The pattern set should be checked to ascertain that it contains the correct number of components for the material which is to be cut.
- If the marker is for open cloth, the pattern set should be verified for correct pairing.
- Each component must be clearly marked with grain lines and direction indicators.
- The direction indicators should be checked against the fabric itself.
- Net width has to be established.
- It would help if the main matching points for checked materials are marked on the relevant pattern components.
- This also applies to the symmetry requirements for checked and striped materials.

When these procedures have been completed the planner or cutter can start the actual planning of the marker, incorporating some or all of the following guidelines:

- If the marker is being planned on marker paper, the first stage is to mark the net width for the estimated length, and a starting line at one end. When the marker is being planned directly on the cloth, one end should be ripped across the weft line so as to show whether the cloth is laying straight or otherwise.
- The largest components should be positioned first and where possible the smaller parts are fitted into the remaining spaces.
- Similarly curved lines should be interlocked when possible (Figure 7.12A).
- The same principle applies to the positioning of angled and straight sections which have corresponding forms (Figure 7.12B).
- When there is a permissible amount of tilt from the grain line, care should be taken that two seams which are to be joined are tilted by the same amount.
- The garment cannot be cut precisely if interlocked parts, especially curved sections, are butted too closely together.
- A tight (efficient) marker is characterised by the small amounts of fabric showing between the components.

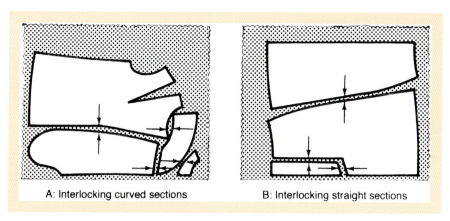

| A: Interlocking curved sections | B: Interlocking straight sections |

Figure 7.12A & B.

Computer Aided Marker Planning

CAD systems are widely used in sample rooms when large numbers of new sample markers have to be produced continuously. Most of these systems have two alternative modes of operation and the choice between them is dictated by the amount of time available for planning and the accessibility of the system during the regular working day. Before starting to plan by either mode, a number of constraints have to be input to the system and these include net width, pile direction, distance between components and the permissible amount of tilt. In addition, the matching points for checked materials also have to be input when necessary. The two modes of operation are interactive and automatic:

- Interactive – This is a two-way electronic communication function between the planner and the system which enables the operator to plan markers with the aid of a computer. During the planning process the system automatically applies the relevant constraints and also indicates to the planner the length of the marker at any given stage. As the system controls all the important details, the planner can concentrate on efficient positioning and reiterations.
- Automatic – When using this mode, another constraint has to be input: the maximum permissible length of the particular marker to be planned. The system plans the markers without any manual intervention and automatically rejects markers which exceed the permissible length. This length is an estimate based on experience and can sometimes lead to the excess usage of materials, but if marker production is more important than a little wastage, the waste has to be accepted. Another benefit of the automatic mode is that markers can be planned overnight without operators being present, thus freeing the system and staff for other productive purposes during the regular working day.

Marker Making

If a CAD system is not used in the sample room, the markers have to be prepared manually. For this two methods can be employed: chalk and paper.

Chalk

This is the simplest and cheapest method but it generally produces inaccurate markers because of the following drawbacks:

- Chalked lines have a tendency to be thick, and thick lines are not conducive to accurate cutting.
- Wax chalk marks remain on the cloth for a reasonable length of time but pipe-clay marks can wholly or partially disappear if the marker is handled often. This could necessitate re-marking or sometimes a little dubious guesswork on the part of the cutter.
- Using undue pressure on the chalk marking can cause some slight distortion of the marked lines, which does not help with the maintenance of accuracy.
- Chalked markers have no real place in a sample room with aspirations towards precision cutting.

Paper

A very accurate method of making markers is to mark the planned pattern arrangement on paper with a fine pen or sharp pencil. There are printed papers specially produced for this purpose, and the two most generally used are:

- Spot and cross (Figure 7.13) – One side of this paper is printed with alternate spot and cross symbols at 2.5 cm spacing in width and length. This print pattern provides the marker planner with very accurate guides for length, width and true bias positioning of components.

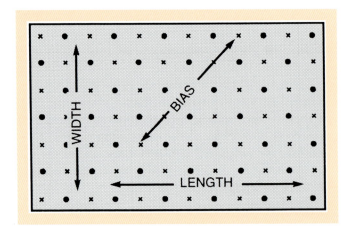

Figure 7.13.

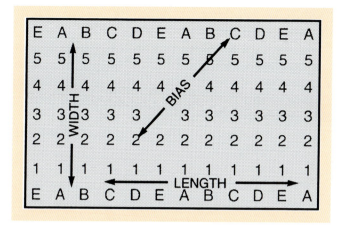

Figure 7.14.

- One-to-five (Figure 7.14) – This marker paper has a print pattern of alternate rows of the letters A to E and the numbers 1 to 5, all at 2.5cm square spacings. The alphanumeric format of this paper gives the planner a high level of visual accuracy control for the placement of patterns.

The advantages of using paper markers are accuracy, the retention of markings and the ease of duplication through wide carbon paper or NCR marker paper.

When completed the paper marker has to be securely affixed to the cloth and there are several methods used for this:

(1) Staples – This method requires a long-arm stapler which can reach within the marker without distorting the lay of the cloth and marker. The staples are positioned in the waste areas of the marker so as to avoid damaging the fabric.
(2) Contact adhesive – This is sprayed onto the cloth and on the underside of the marker. Slight pressure is sufficient to bond the two layers securely.
(3) Heat-seal adhesive – The reverse side of the marker paper is coated with an adhesive and the marker is secured to the cloth by pressing the paper with a light domestic iron, or a large heated plate specially manufactured for this purpose.

The materials used to affix markers are water soluble and they dissolve when the garment is pressed with steam. There could be a problem of residual staining on very fine materials and this should be checked for before deciding how to affix the marker.

Materials Usage

The sample room cannot provide exact figures for materials usage because the amount of material actually required for a garment is somewhat more than the length of the sample marker. Most factories work on a fixed percentage of the marker length, which covers the losses from spreading waste, the elimination of defects, remnants, etc. In practical terms this calculation belongs more to the costing clerk or department than it does to the sample room. What the sample room has to ensure is that:

(1) The sample marker is as efficient as possible
(2) The cost of the material used is within the planned framework for the particular category of garments.

There are factories which require only a fairly accurate estimate from the sample room because they derive materials requirements from multi-size markers which are far more efficient than the single-size markers.

The designer and pattern cutter should also be involved in the marker planning process, and through joint consultation with the marker planner, each marker has to be examined to see whether materials usage can be reduced by pattern modifications. Marker planning is the key factor in materials costs and every centimetre saved is a potential advantage for the company.

CUTTING

Single sample garments can be cut with regular shears or by powered scissors (Figure 7.15) which are just as accurate as shears but are faster and require less physical effort on the part of the cutter. Computerised cutting systems have been developed for single-ply cutting and these are used in sample rooms where large numbers of samples have to be cut continuously.

Figure 7.15.

If the marker is planned on the CAD system it is transferred to the cutting system without the need to plot markers. These systems cut very precisely and the cutting speed is eight to ten times faster than manual methods. Such a system is a substantial investment but a viable one when sample garments have to be produced in large quantities.

Cutting Checks and Stripes
Introduction

Checks and stripes are called, with good reason, problem materials because of the many difficulties involved in their cutting and sewing. This is especially true when there are bold patterns and full matching and symmetry are necessary. There is no one single proven method of cutting these materials because cloth patterns and garment patterns vary considerably and there is always the possibility that the cloth has been distorted during its finishing processes. However, there are some basic techniques and approaches which can be used and they relate to:

(1) The fabric pattern itself
(2) The suitability of the garment pattern
(3) Where to match the cloth pattern
(4) When symmetry is necessary.

The following examples assume that grain lines and pile directions are adhered to, and Figure 7.16 illustrates the main terms used.

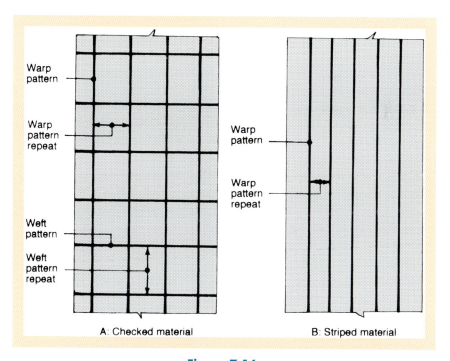

A: Checked material　　　　B: Striped material

Figure 7.16.

Fabric Pattern

This is where it all starts because a decision has to be made as to whether the fabric pattern is:

- bold enough to warrant full matching.
- sufficiently prominent to require partial matching.
- indistinct, and can therefore be safely ignored.

The reasoning is as follows.

Full Matching: This is necessary when there is a conspicuous pattern which, if not matched, would create a visual dissonance on the finished garment. For checked materials and those with prominent weft stripes, this means that the body and sleeves have to be matched all round the garment. These fabrics also require symmetrical elements and sometimes a degree of matching of the warp line pattern.

Partial Matching: This applies mainly to heavily warp striped materials, such as a regularly spaced solid chalk stripe. There are standard features on garments made from these materials which require matching and symmetry and the grain lines play a very important role.

No Matching: If checked or striped materials have a very small pattern motif, there is usually no need for matching or symmetry. What is essential with this type of material is that the grain lines must be strictly observed.

Examples and explanations of matching symmetry are given later in this section.

The Garment Pattern

When planning to make sample garments in checked or striped materials, the designer has to consider whether the intended designs are suitable for the selected materials.

A fabric with a strong pattern is usually the dominant design feature of a garment and, in effect, it is the fabric which is being sold and not seaming and decoration. Therefore it follows that prominent cloth patterns should retain as much of their continuity as possible and not be broken up by seams, darts, etc. In practical terms this means that garment patterns for these materials should contain the minimum number of components which require matching and/or symmetry. A garment design which has a simple assembly will greatly help to minimise the costs of cutting and sewing.

Matching

Although there are a number of similarities in matching checked or striped materials, it is best to consider them individually.

Checks: Cutting these materials has to combine the matching of both the warp and weft patterns and the first question is: where does it start? The size of the warp and weft pattern repeats is the determining factors.

The start – As an example, a typical travel garment would usually have a bulky collar and lapel and the total width of the collar at the centre back is the stand height plus the fall depth. Assuming that the stand height is 5 cm and the fall depth is 9 cm, the fall section of the collar would overlap the back neck seam by 4 cm. With bold patterns it would be preferable to have the weft pattern line running across the centre of the fall section and not positioned close to the outside edge, in order to avoid the possible distortion of the pattern line by irregularities in sewing or pressing. Accordingly, the distance to the next weft stripe down would need to be the measurement of the weft repeat (Figure 7.17). As the position of the first weft stripe on the back has been determined, this will then provide the starting point for matching the front and sleeve.

The same technique can also be used for small weft patterns and close repeats, but care should be taken that the net hem line is not positioned on, or close to, the weft pattern line, so that there is no danger of the cloth pattern line being broken up by mistakes in turning up or pressing the hem.

Sleeves – Irrespective of whether one-piece or split sleeves are being cut, the top section, or visible part, of both sleeves has to match the body. If the sleeve has been correctly constructed vis-à-vis the armhole, the weft matching would start a short distance above the bust line and continue up to the shoulder (Figure 7.18). The objective is to achieve a continuous line around the body and sleeve head even though there are armhole seams.

If the top section of the sleeve is in one piece, the centre line of this section should be positioned on the centre of a warp repeat. For centrally split sleeves

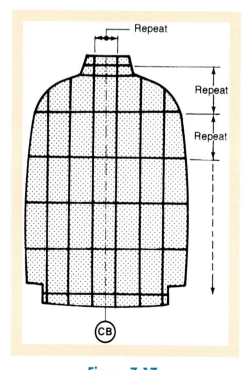

Figure 7.17.

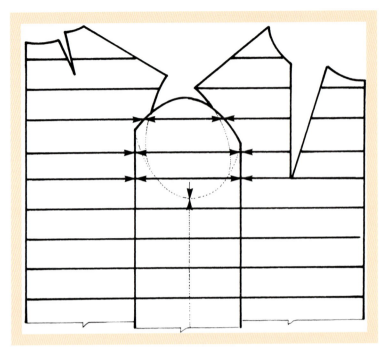

Figure 7.18.

such as raglans or dolmans, both the net centre seams must be positioned on the centre of a warp repeat. When combined, these matching techniques for the warp and weft patterns ensure an unbroken cloth pattern on the top section of the sleeve.

Top collars and backs – The objective of this matching technique is to maintain an unbroken warp pattern down the back, from the crease line of the top collar through to the garment's hem.

If the back is cut in one piece (whole back), the centre back line has to be positioned on the centre of a warp repeat, as is the centre back line of the top collar. Where the back has a centre back seam, the net seam line is also positioned on the centre of a warp repeat (Figure 7.19) and the centre line of the collar is positioned accordingly. Both these instances require that the top collar is both warp and weft matched.

Other components – Other components have to be dealt with on an individual basis and the designer should always consider how the matching requirements can be simplified without affecting the design integrity. The matching of the lapel facings for checked materials is covered later in this chapter in the section on symmetry.

Stripes: Apart from special design features, the matching of warp striped materials is mainly concerned with matching the top collar to the back, and with alignment of the front edges. The other matching requirements for striped materials are those connected with symmetry, dealt with in the next section.

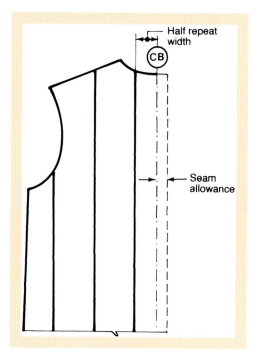

Figure 7.19.

The techniques for matching the centre back section of the top collar to the back are exactly the same as those used for matching the warp pattern of checked materials. The objective is also the same – to ensure the pattern continuity of the entire back section of the garment.

All types of sewn-in sleeves should be positioned according to their grain lines, and pockets such as welts and patches should be matched in the area on which they are located. With patch pockets and flaps on fitted garments, it is not possible to match the entire length of the mouth of the pocket with the body because of waist darts or shaped seams. Under these circumstances, it is acceptable to match only the first two or three stripes from the front edge of the pocket.

What is important for striped materials is that the grain line positioning on the cloth should be as precise as possible. It does not help the appearance of a finished garment if the stripes on adjoining parts give the impression that they are going in opposing directions.

Symmetry

As the majority of garments are symmetrical it follows that the pattern of a material should be positioned symmetrically on the garment. The objective of symmetrical positioning is to make sure that there is a correspondence of the cloth pattern on opposite sides of the garment, i.e. front to front, lapel to lapel, pocket to pocket, etc.

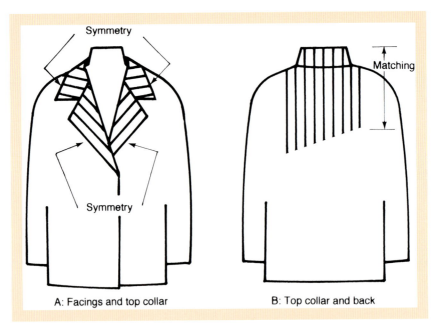

Figure 7.20.

Stripes: The main feature requiring symmetry on garments made from striped materials is the top collar together with the lapel facing (Figure 7.20).

Top collar – The positions of the stripes at the collar ends is a consequence of the positioning of the collar centre back line, and the two collar ends have to be exactly the same. As the collar stripes are at a different angle from those of the facing seam, they cannot be matched along this seam.

Lapel facing – The stripe on the fabric should be parallel to the edge of the lapel, and the distance from the edge to the stripe has to be the same on both sides. It is advisable not to position the stripe too close to the edge in order to prevent it from being broken up by incorrect sewing or pressing.

Checks: Achieving symmetry with checked materials is complicated by the fact that the weft pattern also has to be taken into account. Again, the main feature requiring symmetry is the top collar and the lapel facing and the same principles as with striped materials can be applied to checked materials, with the proviso that the weft stripes on the collar ends and facing are also symmetrical (Figure 7.21). Components such as patch pockets must be symmetrical irrespective of how they are to be matched.

Skirts and Trousers

So far, in the sections dealing with matching and symmetry, examples have been concentrated on body garments because these garments contain all the features necessary to demonstrate the techniques involved. But the clothing industry does not just produce body garments, it also produces skirts and trousers and sometimes these two garments are made from checked and striped materials.

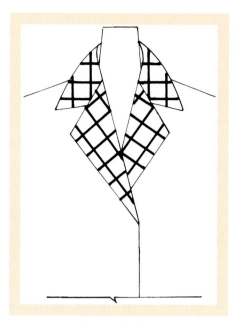

Figure 7.21.

Skirts: Pleats of all kinds are a customary design feature for skirts. When used in designs for checked or striped skirts they can create a problem for the cutting room. Every pleat line on the skirt demands the following procedures:

- Strict observance of grain lines.
- Symmetry of the pleat openings, apart from that for the front and back.
- Maintenance of the fabric design continuity in the areas containing pleats.

When taken together these procedures are costly, and whenever possible the necessity to use them should be kept to a minimum.

As with body garments mentioned earlier, if materials have prominent patterns these are the central design feature of the shirt, and the fabric is the selling focus, not pleats and seaming. So the conclusion for the designer is to keep it simple, because if it is simple it is also quick.

Trousers: As a rule, apart from fabrics and colours, trouser designs concentrate on silhouette and fitting rather than on seaming and decorative effects. This means that matching and symmetry are relatively simple for the cutting room. Grain lines have to be observed, and for checks the pattern on the leg seams has to be matched and the pattern on the seat seam must be symmetrical. If the trousers have flapped or patch pockets, these can be matched to their surrounding areas or in the case of checks the designer has the option of cutting them on the bias. Irrespective of the matching requirements, the fabric pattern on pockets and other visible components should always be symmetrical.

Where matching and symmetry are necessary, it must be accepted that materials usage will be greater than that for garments made in plain fabrics. This increase is slight for stripes but considerable for checked fabrics. However, if for any one season checks are the fashion then the designer has, more than ever, to punctiliously examine every intended design for patterned fabrics in terms of labour and material costs.

CHAPTER **8**

The Principles of Fusing Technology

Every clothing manufacturer continually attempts to produce garments with immediate sales appeal. However, one of the most important materials used for nearly every item of outerwear has no sales appeal, because it is invisible to the consumer. This material is the fusible interlining, and since these materials were first introduced in the early 1950s, they have become an integral component of garment construction.

The term fusible interlining is used to describe a base fabric coated on one side with a thermoplastic adhesive resin which can be bonded to another fabric by the controlled (time) application of heat and pressure. These materials provide the designer with a number of properties which can enhance the appearance of finished garments by the following:

- Control and stabilisation of critical areas
- Strengthening of certain areas such as buttonholes
- Reinforcement of specific design features
- Minimum of modification to the "handle" of the top cloth.

Correctly selected and applied, fusible interlinings have many advantages for the designer, the production unit and the consumer.

CONSTRUCTION OF FUSIBLE INTERLININGS

A fusible interlining combines the following three factors in its construction:

(1) Base material – Also called the substrate
(2) Thermoplastic resins – Synthetic resins which melt when subjected to heat and revert to their original solid state when cooled
(3) Coating – The amount of resin deposited and how it is secured on to the base fabric.

Figure 8.1A shows the basic construction of a fusible interlining and Figure 8.1B illustrates how the resin is disbursed into the top cloth when the two layers are bonded. The finished bond is referred to as a laminate.

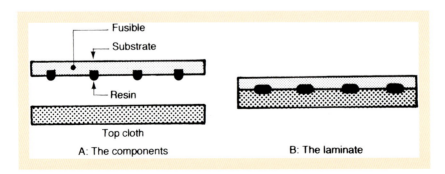

A: The components   B: The laminate

Figure 8.1A & B.

Base Materials

The base materials are produced in a diversity of woven, knitted and nonwoven forms, with each type having its own particular application according to its intended function on the garment. The materials can be produced from natural or synthetic fibres or from blends of each of these fibres. Base cloths influence the following characteristics of the finished garment:

- Handle and bulk
- Shape retention
- Shrinkage control
- Crease recovery
- Appearance after washing or dry cleaning
- Durability.

The properties of different base materials sometimes overlap to a considerable extent so the following descriptions contain some generalisations.

Woven Substrates

Due to their construction, woven substrates are not easily distorted by wear or cleaning and they exert a large degree of control on shrinkage and shape retention; but these properties are not particularly conducive to a soft and natural handle, which is a much sought after attribute for contemporary garments. Developments of twill weaves with fine warp threads and thicker weft threads have improved the handle and bulk properties of this type of base cloth.

Knitted Substrates

Knitted substrates provide a degree of elasticity to the laminate by yielding, together with the top cloth, to body and limb movements. The first knitted substrates were warp knitted (Figure 8.2A), and when weft inserted yarns were introduced into the construction (Figure 8.2B), knitted base cloths became widely accepted for fusing to woven top cloths. A big advantage of a weft-insert substrate

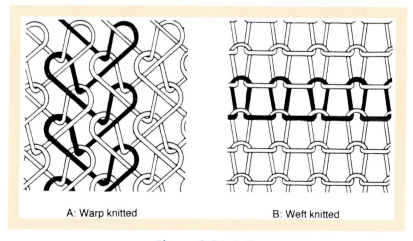

A: Warp knitted   B: Weft knitted

Figure 8.2A & B.

is that it has a natural handle whilst being resilient in the warp direction, i.e. around the body area where it is used. As the knitting process is generally faster than weaving, these materials are cheaper than woven substrates.

Nonwoven Substrates

Nonwoven substrates are made of a series or mixture of fibres held together at bond sites. The fibres can be natural, synthetic or various combinations of the two, but due to the cost of natural fibres, most nonwovens are constructed from synthetic fibres. The most commonly used fibres for general purpose fusible interlining interlinings are viscose, polyester, acrylic and nylon. Nylon fibres tend to produce a relatively firm substrate and are often used when a component requires additional stiffening.

The orientation of the fibres in the substrate influences its end use. The three standard web formations are:

(1) Random (Figure 8.3A) – The fibres are orientated randomly and the resultant substrate is omnidirectional. This property helps with material utilisation but the fusible interlining itself lacks strength and resilience in any one direction.

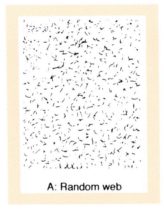

A: Random web

Figure 8.3A.

(2) Parallel (Figure 8.3B) – As the name implies, the fibres are orientated to the length of substrate which makes this fusible interlining ideal for preventing stretching.

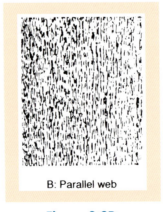

B: Parallel web

Figure 8.3B.

(3) Cross-laid (Figure 8.3C) – In this web, the fibres are orientated at an angle of 45° across the substrate, which gives the opportunity of cutting components on the true bias or on the straight.

C: Cross-laid web

Figure 8.3C.

Resins

Resins are the sole bonding agent between the top cloth and substrate and irrespective of the type of resin used; they have to conform to the following conditions:

Upper-limit temperature – The resin should become viscous at a temperature below that which would damage the top cloth. Whilst this temperature varies according to the composition of the top cloth, it rarely exceeds 175° C.

Lower-limit temperature – This is the lowest temperature at which the resin starts to become viscous. For most fusible interlining this is about 110° C, and for the fusible interlinings used for leather and suede materials, the temperature is considerably lower.

Cleanability – The adhesive properties of the resin have to be sufficiently strong to withstand washing and/or dry cleaning throughout the normal life of the garment.

Handle – The resin must contribute to the required handle and not act as an unwanted stiffening agent on the final laminate.

Resin Types and Applications

The types and properties of the most widely used resins are:

Polyethylene – At different densities this is suitable for wash and wear garments or for those which have to be dry cleaned only.

Polyamide – All polyamide resins produce full dry cleanable and washable bonds but there is a class of this resin which is dry cleanable only.

Polyester – These resins have the same general properties as polyamides but are generally a little cheaper.

PVC – Used extensively for siliconised rainwear fabrics.

Table 8.1.

Resin type	Fusing system		Durability		Relative cost
	Steam	Electric	Wash	Dry Clean	
Polyethelene (low density)	limted	good	suitable	limited	low
Polyethelene (high density)	not recommended	good	good	good	medium
Polyamides	good	good	limited	good	high
Polyester	good	good	limited	good	medium
Plasticised C.A.	good	good	suitable	suitable	medium
Phenolics	limted	good	limited	suitable	medium

Plasticised cellulose acetate – A multi-purpose resin which is both washable and dry cleanable.

Plasticised polyvinyl acetate – Mainly used for leather and fur materials but is not dry cleanable and has very limited washability.

The general characteristics of these resins are summed up in Table 8.1.

Coating

There are two aspects of the coating: density and coating system.

Density

Resins are applied to substrates in three different densities – low, medium and high – and the degree of density refers to the actual mass per unit volume of the resin material. This physical density is directly related to the melting point of the resin and its resistance to dry cleaning solvents, and as a rule the higher the density, the better the resin stands up to dry cleaning.

Coating System

This refers to the process whereby the resin is deposited and secured on the substrate. There are three principal methods:

(1) Scatter coating – This method uses electronically controlled scattering heads to deposit the resin crystals on to the moving substrate. The drawback of this method is that the substrate surface is covered with resin, which reduces the flexibility of the laminate.

(2) Dry dot printing – In this process the resin is printed on to the substrate in regularly spaced dots by means of rollers with indentations which hold the resin crystals. This method is generally regarded as producing the most flexible bond.

(3) Preformed – The resin is heat processed to form a net which is then bonded onto the substrate by heat and pressure. During heating the link lines of the

net melt, leaving a minute dot pattern on the base cloth. This method is also used to produce paper-backed tapes which are used for fastening hems and facings instead of blindstitching or felling.

FUSING PROCESS

Regardless of which fusible interlining and machine are used, fusing is controlled by four processing components – temperature, time, pressure and cooling – and these have to be accurately combined in order to achieve the optimum results.

Temperature

There is a limited range of temperatures that are effective for each type of resin. Too high a temperature causes the resin to become too viscous, which could result in the resin being forced through to the right side of the cloth – known as bleed through or strike through. If the temperature is too low, the resin is not sufficiently viscous to disburse into the top cloth. In general, resin-melt temperatures range from 130°–160°C and the best results will normally occur within +78°C of the temperature specified by the manufacturer of the fusible interlining.

Time

The only time element of any value during the fusing process is when the top cloth and fusible interlining are under pressure in the heating zone of the machine. This time cycle for a particular fusible interlining is determined by:

• Whether the fusible interlining has a high- or low-melt resin.
• If a light or heavy substrate is being used.
• The nature of the top cloth being used, i.e. thick or thin, dense or open.

Manufacturers of fusible interlinings supply data sheets which give the time cycle for each fusible interlining, and this refers to the actual fusing stage only.

Pressure

When the resin is viscous, pressure is applied to the top cloth and fusible interlining assembly to ensure that:

• Full contact is made between the top cloth and fusible interlining.
• Heat transfer is at the optimum level.
• There is an even penetration of the viscous resin into the fibres of the top cloth.

Most fusing machines use two steel rollers or pressure plates to create pressure, but a flexible pressure system has been developed which automatically adapts itself to variations in the thickness of the assembly being fused, whilst maintaining an even pressure over the entire assembly.

Cooling

Enforced cooling is used so that the fused assemblies can be handled immediately after fusing. Cooling can be induced by various systems, including water-cooled plates, compressed air circulation and vacuum. Rapidly cooling the fused assemblies to 30°–35°C makes for a higher level of productivity than if operators have to wait for the assemblies to cool naturally.

FUSING MACHINERY

A press is used for fusing and three basic types are:

(1) Steam press
(2) Flat bed press
(3) Conveyor belt press.

Each type of machine has its own range of capabilities.

Steam Press

Regular steam pressing machines are not designed for fusing. Although some fusible interlinings are produced for use on these machines it is inadvisable to use them. These machines have some serious limitations regarding fusing, including:

- Inability to reach the heat levels required by the majority of resins.
- The shape and size of the bucks restrict the size of the components which can be fused.
- Most utility machines are not fitted with programme controls, which means that the entire process is operator controlled.
- If the resin was originally activated by steam heat, the same thing can happen when garments are pressed during their production. This situation can cause serious problems with the stability of the laminates.
- Regular steam pressing machines have serious shortcomings for this application and should not be used for fusing.

Flat Bed Press

Flat bed presses are purpose built fusing machines produced in a large variety of sizes and with many types of work aids. This type of press has padded top and bottom bucks with electric heating elements in one or both bucks. The bottom buck is static and the top buck is lowered to fuse the assembly whilst under pressure, and then raised after cooling. Most of these machines are fitted with timers and programme controls and can achieve high levels of fusing quality.

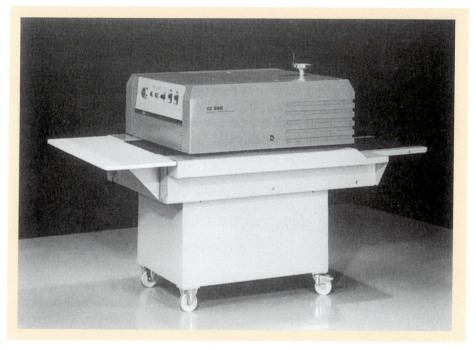

Figure 8.4.

Conveyor Belt Press

Conveyor belt presses are also called continuous machines because they can be operated without stopping for the loading and unloading of the assemblies. The conveyor belt transports the assemblies through all the processes and the belt speed is adjustable according to the time cycle required. This type of machine is available in different lengths and widths and can be fitted with automatic feeding and unloading systems. These machines may well be microprocessor controlled.

The compact machine shown in Figure 8.4 is designed to fuse the small quantities which are produced in the sample room. It has exactly the same range of fusing characteristics as its industrial big brother and can be fitted with a return feed system and stacker if its production has to be increased. A feature of the machine illustrated is that one side is open so as to allow for the partial fusing of wider components, such as coat foreparts.

THE SELECTION OF FUSIBLE INTERLININGS

While the selection of fusible interlinings involves some subjective factors, it does not preclude the use of a systematic and objective selection procedure which covers the following factors.

Top Cloth

It should never be assumed that fusing is possible for every cloth without checking the following points:

- Will the fusing process produce excessive shrinkage, glazing or permanent colour change?
- Does the top cloth have a siliconised finish which would adversely affect fusing quality?
- Some fabrics constructed from continuous filament yarns can be problematic as regards fusing. Trials are advisable.
- Does the top cloth have an open construction that will show the resin on the right side?
- Is there a pile, nap or raised pattern on the top cloth which could be damaged by the pressure used during the fusing process?

Apart from the above points, it is always worth checking the handle and draping qualities of the cloth after fusing.

Base Cloths

Fusible interlinings could be woven, knitted or nonwoven of varying weights, with nonwovens being most popular due to minimum wastage during cutting and overall lower cost. Different parts of the same garment could require the use of different fusible interlinings, so the evaluation of suitability should take into account the function of the fusible interlining in relation to the area and/or component to be fused. Nonwoven fusible interlinings are predominantly used for small area reinforcements such as pockets, vent edges, hems and under collars as well as larger areas of the garment. Because the choice of base fabric in the fusible interlining is made in relation to the characteristics of the main fabric, areas requiring more uniform extension would use a knitted fusible interlining. Cost, as ever, has an influence and the more expensive end of the market would make use of woven fusible interlinings, which add value to the feel and handle of the garment.

Resins

This concerns whether the garment will be dry cleaned or washed, or both. The method used to clean a garment is generally determined by the properties of the top cloth, and the resin used has to match these properties.

Cost

Cost is very important, but it should not necessarily be the sole criterion for selecting a fusible interlining because price itself means very little unless compared to performance. The designer should always verify whether a particular fusible interlining will enhance or degrade the design objectives of the garment.

Remember that an all-purpose fusible interlining which suits every type of fabric and can be fused without any control over temperature, time and pressure has yet to be invented.

PATTERNS FOR FUSIBLE INTERLININGS

Grain Lines

Unless there are compelling reasons to do otherwise, the grain lines of knitted or woven fusible interlinings should be the same as the cloth component for which the fusible interlining is intended (Figure 8.5). For nonwoven fusible interlinings, the grain lines very much depend on the fibre orientation of the material being used and the function of the piece to be cut. If the nonwoven fusible interlining has a definite fibre lay, the resultant grain line can be utilised to advantage when necessary. When the fusible interlining is omnidirectional and has to be used, then needs must, etc.

Seams

With the exception of armholes, shoulder seams, collar and front edges, together with edges of flaps etc, the fusible interlining could be cut back from all seams which have to be pressed open (Figure 8.6) or, alternatively, cut back just sufficiently to allow the fusible interlining to be incorporated into the stitching. In the first instance the amount of the cut-back is the width of the seam allowance plus 1 or 2 mm. This reduces the final thickness of the seam and slightly lessens the degree of accuracy required by the operator when positioning the fusible interlining on the cloth.

Folded Edges

When folds have to be made on fused cloth components, it is advantageous to extend the fusible interlining for about 1.5 cm past the fold line (Figure 8.7). When folded, this extension prevents stretching and helps to maintain a straight fold line as well as preventing the cut edge of the fusible interlining wearing through the folded edge of the main fabric.

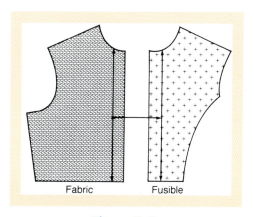

Fabric   Fusible

Figure 8.5.

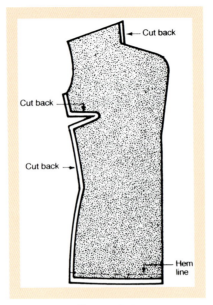

Figure 8.6.

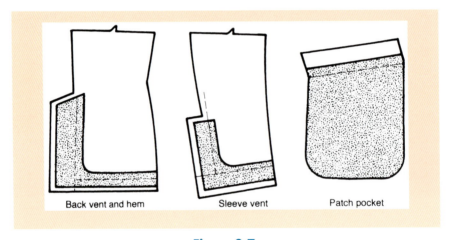

Back vent and hem   Sleeve vent   Patch pocket

Figure 8.7.

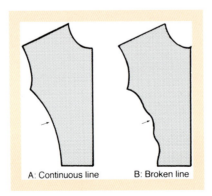

A: Continuous line   B: Broken line

Figure 8.8.

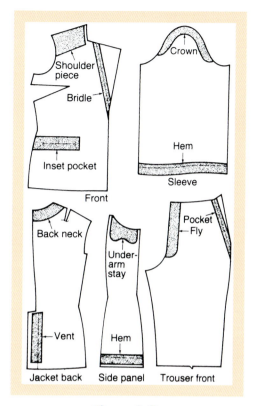

Figure 8.9.

Line Breaking

On fronts that are not fully fused, the impression of the edge of the fusible interlining can often be seen on the right side of the front. In most cases this can be
eliminated by cutting the offending edge in a wave pattern instead of an unbroken
line (Figure 8.8). This procedure can also be used on other components if the same
problem occurs.

Reinforcements

These are used for a variety of applications and their main purpose is to prevent
the stretching of body and sleeve hems, inset pockets, trouser flies, side pockets,
etc (Figure 8.9). Nonwoven fusible interlinings can be used for this purpose
although it is also possible to utilise the waste areas of markers for woven and
knitted fusible interlinings if the grain lines can be observed. Another point to
consider is whether to cut reinforcement components in one size only because this
is a simple and labour-saving method of working.

CHAPTER 9

The Principles of Sewing Technology

Although ultrasonic welding and resin bonding systems have been developed as alternative forms, sewing still remains the most predominant method of assembling garments of all types. In every sector of the clothing industry, sewing operations are performed by a great variety of machines, each of which has the capability for specific operations on a particular category of garments and/or fabric. This wide choice of sewing machinery is also matched by those for sewing threads, needles and other auxiliary components.

In practice the word sewing covers a large number of subjects and it is only when there is a correct balance between all of them that the optimum results can be achieved. This chapter will examine the principles involved.

THE COMPONENTS OF SEWING

Irrespective of type, all sewing machines function in a similar way and the best example for illustrating these elements is the regular sewing machine. There are five basic components of sewing (Figure 9.1): needle, throat plate, presser foot, feed dogs and threads.

Needles

Needles have been used for hand sewing since about 1800 BC and were originally made from ivory, bone, wood and horn (Figure 9.2). Their form has remained unchanged since then. During the 15th century iron needles were introduced for

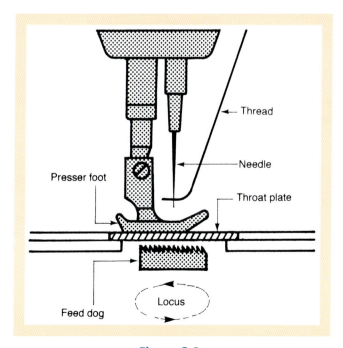

Figure 9.1.

Figure 9.2.

hand sewing, and in 1800 Balthasar Krems of Germany was the first to use a needle with the eye near the point for a chainstitch machine he had developed. The large scale production of sewing machines started in about 1840 and this was paralleled by numerous developments in the manufacture and quality of machine needles. Today the steel needle in common use is a precision product which is critical to the formation of stitches.

The functions of the sewing machine needle are to form a passage in the material through which the needle thread can wholly or partially pass and form a loop which can be picked up by the looper or hook mechanisms. Needles are made in straight or curved forms and their main construction features are (Figures 9.3 and 9.4):

Butt – The truncated conical shape at the top of the needle which facilitates its insertion into the needle bar or clamp.
Shank – Usually larger in diameter than the rest of the needle, the shank can be cylindrical in shape or flat on one side, depending on the method used to secure the needle in or on the needle bar.
Shoulder – The section joining the shank to the blade.
Blade – The longest section of the needle, this runs from the shoulder to the eye.
Long groove and short groove – On one side of the needle there is a long groove which protects the needle thread as it enters and is withdrawn from the fabric. There is a short groove on the opposite side which extends a short distance above and below the eye and its purpose is to aid the passage of the thread into the material and loop formation.

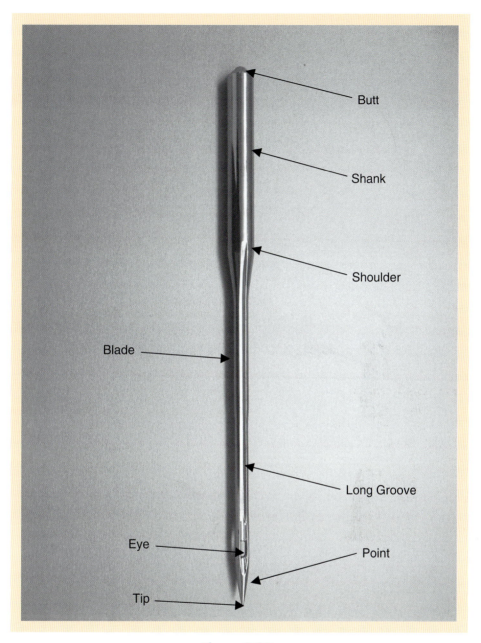

Butt

Shank

Shoulder

Blade

Long Groove

Eye

Point

Tip

Figure 9.3A.

Scarf (Figure 9.4) – This part of the needle has a flattened area that allows the sewing mechanism to pick up the sewing thread in a controlled manner.

Eye – An elliptical hole between the two grooves; the shape and finish of the inside top of the eye are important factors in the prevention of thread damage during sewing.

Point – This is shaped to provide the best penetration of the material being sewn.

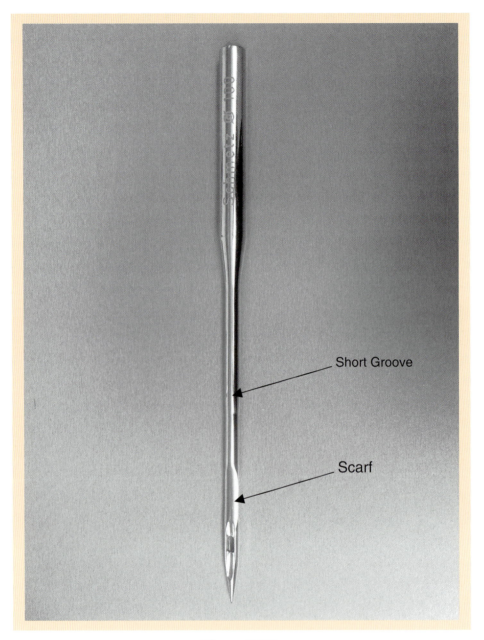

Figure 9.3B.

Tip – The tip, when combined with the point, determines the ease and extent of penetration into the fabric.

Points and tips have a decisive bearing on the performance of the needle and the various types of combinations can be divided into two groups:

Round points – These are used for the sewing of textile materials and whilst they all have a circular cross section, they differ in their tip shapes. In general,

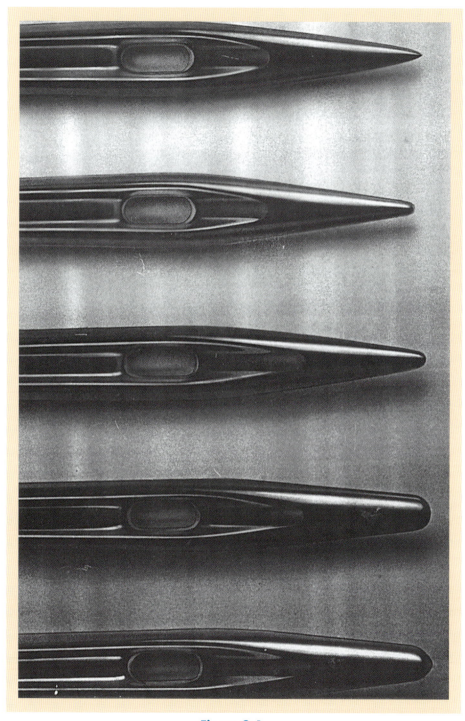

Figure 9.4.

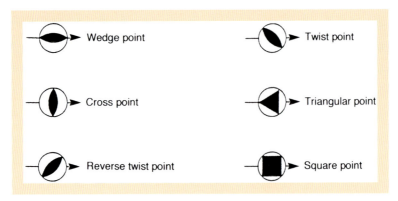

Figure 9.5.

set point needles are used for most woven fabrics and the ball point needle is preferred for delicate and knitted materials. Both these points are available with light, medium and heavy tips (Figure 9.4) and these combinations allow for good compatibility between the fabric and the needle.

Cutting points – These needles actually cut a hole through the material and because of this are mainly used for the sewing of leather, artificial leather and plastic materials. The points come in a variety of shapes (Figure 9.5). They all influence the set (angle) of the stitches and as a result the appearance of a row of stitches. The individual stitches are slightly slanted instead of being in a straight line.

Sizes

There are about 20 systems of designating needle size but the one used most widely is the metric system (Nm). This is based on the diameter of the blade multiplied by 100. For example, a needle with a blade diameter of 0.9 mm would be size Nm 90. Although needle lengths for each type of machine are standardised, longer needles are sometimes used to increase the clearance between the end of the needle bar and the work being sewn.

Some modern sewing machines can reach speeds in excess of 10 000 revolutions/stitches per minute. With chainstitch machines, one stitch is formed with each revolution. On lockstitch machines, one stitch is formed with two revolutions. Hence on lockstitch machines with a top speed of 5000 rpm, 2500 stitches are formed per minute. At these speeds, plus the immense range of different materials which have to be sewn, the selection of the correct needle is crucial.

Throat Plate (Figure 9.6)

The throat plate is a static component which has slots for the feed dogs, and one or more holes for needles or a slot for swing-needle machines such as a zigzag. The upper surface of the throat plate is highly polished so as to enable the material to slide over this area as smoothly as possible.

Presser Foot (Figure 9.7)

The presser foot is attached to the pressure bar of the machine and its two prime purposes are to:

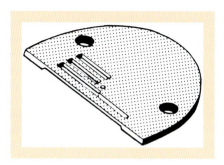

Figure 9.6.

Hold the material securely against the throat plate and prevent it shifting during the movement of the needle.

Maintain a slight pressure contact between the material and the feed dogs to ensure that material moves at the same rate and direction as the feed dogs themselves.

Apart from the standard presser foot, there are special purpose feet which help the operator perform operations other than regular seaming. Amongst others, there are feet for piping edges, zip setting, cording, tape-binding, hemming, and those which incorporate guides for top stitching.

Feed Dogs (Figure 9.8)

The basic function of the feed dogs is to move the fabric forward by a distance equal to the stitch length, between successive penetrations of the needle. The feed dog itself can have one or more raised rows of serrated teeth which rise through the slots in the throat plate and slightly enmesh with the underside of the fabric. Feed dogs have an elliptical locus (movement) and this advances the material the necessary distance; the feed dogs then drop below the surface of the throat plate and are positioned ready for the next cycle. There are many types of feed dogs and feed systems and the principal ones are examined later in this chapter.

Figure 9.7.

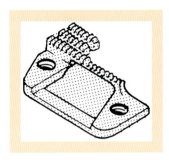

Figure 9.8.

Sewing Threads (Figure 9.9)

Almost all garments produced have one component in common: the sewing thread. Whilst sewing threads are usually a relatively small percentage of the cost of a garment, they have an extremely significant influence on the appearance and durability of the finished product. The production of sewing threads is an extensive and complex subject, and the reader would do well to refer to *The Technology of Thread and Seams* published by Coats Ltd for a detailed coverage of the processes involved.

In practical terms, any examination of sewing threads must start with the question, what are the essential requirements for a sewing thread? The answers can be grouped under two headings, sewability and durability.

Sewability

This describes the basic all-round properties of the thread, including:

- Not breaking when used for high-speed sewing.
- Facilitating the consistent formation of stitches.
- The minimum occurrence of skipped stitches.

In order to prevent changes in tension during sewing, the thread must have a uniform diameter.

A high level of resistance to abrasion is essential due to the friction of the thread in the needle eye and with other mechanisms.

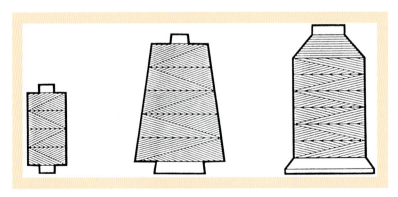

Figure 9.9.

The thread has to have sufficient surface smoothness to pass easily through the guides on the machine. This ensures the uniformity of stitch formation.

Durability

The main thread related factors under this heading are:

- The thread has to have sufficient elasticity to withstand the normal pressures imposed on seams during wear. This is particularly important for knitted fabrics because of their inherent extensibility.
- Thread shrinkage should be minimal after the garment has been washed or dry cleaned. Seam puckering is often caused by unstable thread.

It is important that the thread maintains its original colour after being subjected to cleaning processes. In particular, this applies to the threads used for top stitching and other decorative purposes such as embroidery.

Thread Types

Ideally a sewing thread should combine the best properties of sewability and durability, and whilst there are many threads available which approach this, certain compromises have to be accepted due to various technical limitations. However, for practical purposes sewing threads for the clothing industry can be divided into three broad groups: cotton, synthetics and corespun.

Cotton: Threads made from cotton fibres have excellent sewability because the fibres are very supple and are not seriously affected by the heat generated by needles during sewing. On the other hand, cotton threads are not highly durable and some of the softer types have a tendency to shrink when the garment is washed. Glace and mercerised cotton threads sew well and have a lustrous appearance, but they both shrink slightly when wetted.

Synthetics: This is a large group of threads made mainly from nylon, polyester rayon and polyamide filaments or fibres. The threads are very durable and are not affected by moisture or the chemicals used in washing powders or dry cleaning solvents. In addition, they have excellent dimensional stability and a high level of resistance to abrasion. Synthetic threads are available in a number of different constructions and finishes, which enhances their performance for special sewing applications.

Corespun (Figure 9.10): This thread has a continuous filament polyester core wrapped in cotton fibres, which produces a strong thread with excellent sewability. Corespun threads have good elasticity and a high resistance to heat and shrinkage, but cost more than regular threads because they have to be dyed twice, first for the polyester core and then for the cotton wrap. An advantage of corespun threads is that finer threads can be used due to the superior strength of the polyester core.

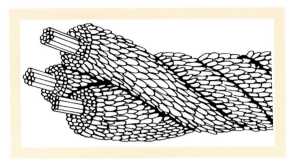

Figure 9.10.

Other Fibres: Two other natural fibre threads which have limited applications are silk and linen.

Silk – These threads are strong, with good elongation and a highly lustrous appearance. Silk threads have good sewability but the high cost restricts their use for mass production sewing.

Linen – Once widely used for sewing tents, shoes, leather etc, threads spun from flax have been mostly replaced by synthetics.

A summary of the main characteristics of various types of threads is given in Table 9.1 but selection also has to take into account the fabric and its finish, needle size, stitch type, seam construction and the sewing speed.

Thread Sizes

There are many systems for defining thread size but the most widely used is the Tex number system. This is based on the gram weight of 1000 m of yarn, so a fine thread would have a low Tex number and a thick thread would have a high number. Thread manufacturers using other systems will normally provide the Tex equivalent values.

Costs

Price is not necessarily the sole criterion for purchasing sewing threads because it is performance which really counts. Trouble-free sewing combined with durability is essential to prevent constant work stoppages caused by continual breaks, and to avoid consumer dissatisfaction with seams that open during normal wear conditions.

Feed Systems

Feed systems relate to the combination of the needle, throat plate, presser foot and feed dogs which control the feed of the material from stitch to stitch whilst regulating the relationship between the plies being sewn. Some examples are given here.

Table 9.1.

Property/type	Sewabiltiy	Durability	Strength	Suppleness	Abrasion resistance	Heat resistance	Colour resistance	Shrinkage resistance	Elasticity
Cotton	High	Moderate	High	Moderate	High	Good	Moderate	Moderate	
Soft cotton	High	Moderate	High	Moderate	High	Good	Low	Moderate	
Glace cotton	High	Moderate	Good	Good	High	Good	Moderate	Moderate	
Mercerised cotton	Moderate	Moderate	High	Good	High	High	Good	High	Good
Polyester	Moderate	High	Good	High	Good	High	High	Good	
Polyamide (nylon)	Moderate	High	High	Good	High	Moderate	Good	High	High
Polyester cotton	High	High	High	High	Good	High	Good	High	High
Core-spun	Very high	High	High	Good	Good	Good	High	Good	High

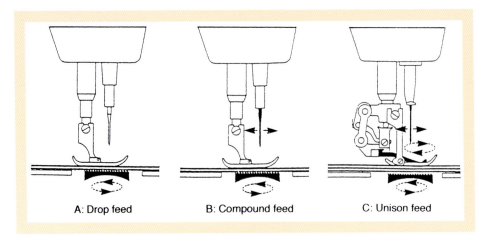

A: Drop feed   B: Compound feed   C: Unison feed

Figure 9.11.

Drop feed (Figure 9.11A)

This is the most common feeding system used in apparel manufacture and the most cost effective. A disadvantage of this feed is that the material being fed through the machine is reliant upon the feed feeding both plies of the fabric simultaneously. Depending upon the properties of the material, there are instances when the presser foot can push the top ply resulting in fabric and seam distortion.

Compound feed (Figure 9.11B)

A disadvantage of this feed system is because the fabric is pinned together by the needle and the feed, it is very difficult to reposition the fabric during sewing.

Unison feed (Figure 9.11C)

The complex nature of these mechanisms and a greater number of moving parts usually results in much slower sewing speeds.

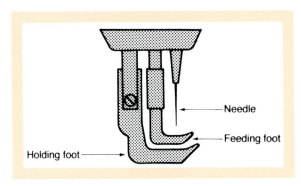

Needle

Feeding foot

Holding foot

Figure 9.12.

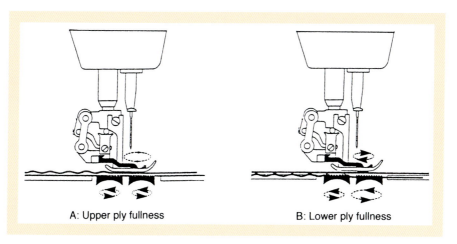

A: Upper ply fullness   B: Lower ply fullness

Figure 9.13.

Differential feed (Figure 9.13)

These systems have two independently operated feed dogs, one behind and one in front of the needle. The feed dogs can be regulated so as to create fullness on the upper or lower ply of the seam; for example, easing the back shoulder seam onto the front shoulder seam.

There are also a number of mechanisms which are used as auxiliary feed systems where there are special feed requirements, such as embroidery machines and automatic long-seamers used for closing the leg seams of trousers.

STITCHES AND SEAMS

Stitches and seams are the basic elements of sewing, and national and international standards have been developed for accurately classifying them. Some examples are given here.

Stitches

The basic classes in British Standard 3870 Part 1 are:

Class 100 – These are chainstitches formed from a needle thread only and they are typically used for basting, felling and blindstitching

Class 200 – Originally hand stitches; these are mostly formed by single threads passed from one side of the material to the other with each successive penetration of the needle. Various classes of this stitch are used for saddle stitching and the prick stitching of edges.

Class 300 – These are also referred to as lock stitches because the top and under groups of threads are interlaced to form the stitch. The most widely used

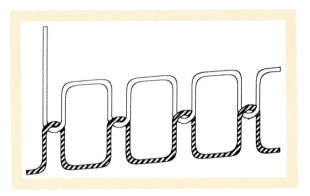

Figure 9.14.

stitch formation in this class is no. 301 (Figure 9.14), which is that produced
by a regular sewing machine.

Class 400 – Formed by two or more groups of threads, the loops of which are
interlooped, stitch no. 401 (Figure 9.15) is a chainstitch formed from two
threads and is widely used for knitted materials because the stitch formation
makes for good extensibility and lateral strength.

Class 500 – These are known as overedge (overlock) stitches because at least one
group of threads covers the edge of the material. In this class, stitch no. 504
(Figure 9.16) is a three-thread overlocking stitch used for assembling light weight
knits and also for cleaning and finishing the seam and hem edges of garments.

When the 401 chainstitch and the 504 overlock stitch are sewn simultaneously they form what is called a five-thread safety stitch where the chain and overlock stitches are not connected. This stitch combination is widely used for seaming
denim and cheaper grades of trousers. Another class of safety stitch, sometimes called
a mock safety stitch, is formed from four threads where one or two of the overlock
threads interlace with the needle thread. This stitch class is used for assembling garments made from light weight materials and sometimes for linings. Due to their construction, safety stitched seams cannot be pressed open but have to be pressed to one
side which, with heavy weight materials, is apt to create a bulky seam appearance.

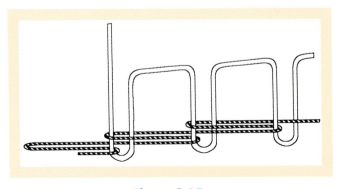

Figure 9.15.

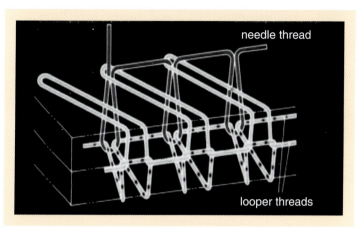

needle thread

looper threads

Figure 9.16.

Class 600 – There are many complex stitch formations in this class because the stitches can be formed from three to nine threads and the use of up to four needles. This class of stitches is characterised by high elasticity and strength and is frequently used for flat butted seams in the corsetry and underwear sectors of the clothing industry.

Seams

British Standard 3870:1991 classifies seam constructions under eight headings. Typical examples are given here and shown in Figure 9.17.

Class 1 – Superimposed seams: This seam is constructed with a minimum of two components and is the most widely used seam construction in this class. Among others, safety stitched and French seams are covered by this class.

Class 2 – Lapped seams: The best example of this class is the lapped seam construction used for many denim articles and for certain types of blouses and shirts.

Class 3 – Bound seams: Used for constructing a decorative edge binding from self or other material such as tape.

Class 4 – Flat seams: In this class the seam edges do not overlap but are butted together.

Class 5 – Decorative seams: This construction consists of a row or rows of stitches sewn through one or more plies of fabric. The channel seam shown in Figure 9.17 is representative of this class.

Class 6 – Edge neatening: This could refer to the overlocked edge of a single ply or to the single turned overlocked hem of a blouse.

Class 7 – These are sometimes called applied seams because they are mainly used to apply a decorative material to an edge or seam, such as the lace edging on a nightdress sleeve.

Class 8 – Constructed from one ply of fabric only, this class is commonly used for belts and belt loops. Figure 9.17 illustrates one version of this class whereby the waist band is simultaneously folded and stitched onto the waist line of a skirt.

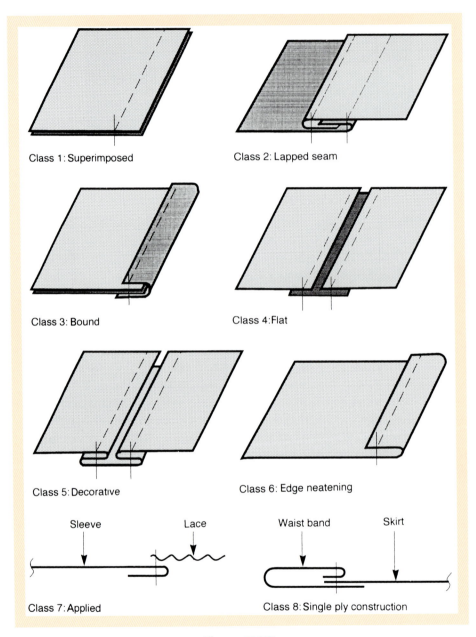

Figure 9.17.

Standard classifications for stitches and seams are indispensable because apart from reducing ambiguity in communication, the definitions enable a more precise focus to be made when considering these two fundamental elements of sewing.

MACHINERY AND EQUIPMENT

Since the mid 1980s many technological advances have been made to the sewing machinery which is used for the production of clothing. New construction materials and improved electronic systems have played an important role in these advances. They include:

"Dry-machines" – These machines are manufactured with sealed anti-friction bearings which eliminates oil changes during the normal working life of the machine.

Variable speed electronic motors – Machines such as bartackers and automatic seamers have to sew over considerably different thicknesses of materials and seam constructions. Where the machine had one sewing speed only, snapped threads and broken needles were a frequent occurrence when sewing over varying thicknesses. It is now possible to adjust the machine's sewing speed according to what has to be sewn, and this capability makes a positive contribution to the improvement of productivity.

Integrated motor – Instead of the drive motor being mounted separately under the table, it is now integrated with the machine head as one unit.

User Friendly

Sewing machine manufacturers are now seriously taking into account the operators who will use their machines and are incorporating many of the following items into their designs.

Machines now have large clearances in their main working areas, which facilitates the easy and comfortable manipulation of work during sewing. The positions and shapes of a machine's control elements are ergonomically designed so as to suit the natural movement range and convenience of the operator.

In accordance with new safety regulations, machines have built-in safety devices which protect the operator and the machine against operational errors.

Specially designed stands are available for machines where the operator works in a standing instead of a seated position. The standing working position is a distinctive feature of quick-response types of production systems.

Machines are painted in colours that are easy on the eye and which fit in with the dynamic colour schemes used in modern factories.

These are just a few of the innovations which, with many others, are gradually becoming standard features for all types of sewing machines.

Basic Machines

A comprehensive review of all the different machines on the market is beyond the scope of this book, but the following are some of the machines most widely used for the production of clothing.

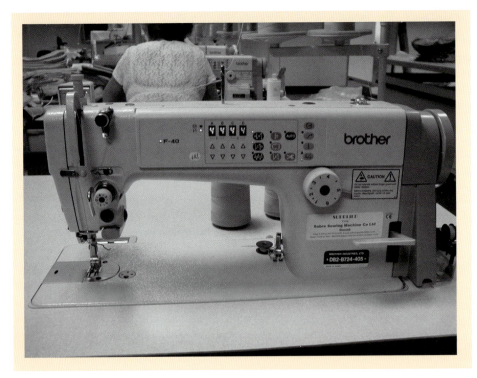

Figure 9.18.

Integrated Sewing Unit (ISU Figure 9.18)

This machine is the basic workhorse of the clothing industry and has numerous applications due to the great variety of work aids and feed systems available for it. Some of the main features of this class of machine are:

They are generally available in three versions for sewing light, medium or heavy weight materials.

With the addition of a programmable microprocessor control system, the machine can be programmed for repetitive operations such as sewing around labels or stitching simple decorative elements.

Many versions of this machine have bobbins which hold 50% more thread than the conventional bobbin. An electronic monitoring system ensures that when the bobbin is changed, no seam interruption is visible on the top part of the side being sewn.

Electronically controlled thread cutting, tacking, needle positioning and foot lifting systems have become standard equipment on these and many other machines.

Three-thread Overlock with a Microprocessor (Figure 9.19)

Based on a regular overlock machine, this version is used for the assembly seaming of garments made up in light weight knitted materials. The microprocessor enables the accurate calibration of stitch tension without manually adjusting the spring

Figure 9.19.

tensioners, and permits automatic cutting of the thread chain at the beginning and end of seams. A "tractor-foot" can be fitted to this machine when sewing seams with varying thicknesses.

Automating the Sewing Process

These comprise of machines by which, machine processing of a product is achieved with little, or no human intervention. Another definition is that of production that is machine driven. The class of machine described above is now classed as a basic sewing machine but it still has electronic technology that enables sophisticated actions such as automatic presser foot lifting and automatic thread trimming to be performed. The evolution of sewing machine technology has progressed further to enable even greater advances in apparel production. The advantages of machine automation are:

- Machine performing tasks reduces/eliminates operator fatigue.
- A possible reduction in labour costs.
- Production more streamlined and efficient.
- Reduced human intervention improves the quality of the product.

   Disadvantages with machine automation are:

- The dexterity of fingertips in manipulating fabrics for sewing cannot, at this time, be managed by mechanical means.

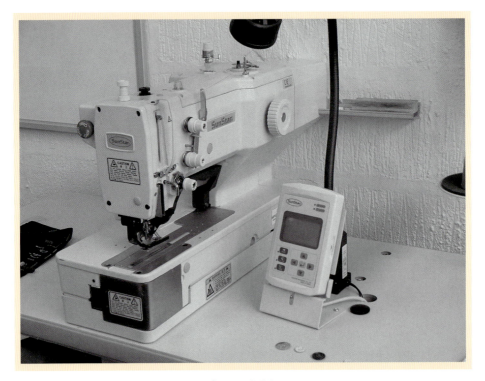

Figure 9.20.

- The flexible structure of textiles makes it more difficult to handle fabrics when sewing.
- Textile materials tend to stick together and can be difficult to separate.
- Production flexibility is more difficult with regard to changing over to new styles/products.

Machine automation has been split into two categories of mechanised sewing and semi-automatic sewing.

Mechanised Sewing Machines: These are machines which still require the operator to place and control parts within the sewing area but sew a pre-determined stitch line or pattern.
   Examples of these are:

- Bar tack machines.
- Button hole machines.
- Button sewing machines.
- Spot tack machines.

Lockstitch Bartacker (Figure 9.21): This class of machine has a wide range of applications apart from regular bartacking operations. It can easily be converted to sew an endless variety of stitch patterns in an area 6 cm × 6 cm where the

Figure 9.21.

pattern contains up to 72 stitches. Sewing speed is adjustable according to the thickness of the part being sewn, and the free cylinder arm makes handling easier when bartacking on cylindrical sections of garments such as belt loops, pocket corners and trouser flies.

Lockstitch Buttonhole Machine (Figure 9.20): The machine illustrated is for sewing buttonholes in light weight materials, such as those used for blouses, dresses and shirts. In one continuous operation the machine sews a rectangular shaped buttonhole by means of purl-stitch, and both ends are secured by a bartack. The machine is operated by one pedal only and the head can be mounted in the length or across the width of the work top, depending on whether vertical or horizontal buttonholes are being sewn.

Blind Stitch Machines: These machines are available in different versions for blindstitching the hems and facings of garments made in materials ranging from sheer to heavy weight. The machine forms a single-thread stitch and can sew up to 3000 stitches per minute. Stitch penetration control is digitally displayed and most machines are fitted with thread trimmers and a stitch condensing device which prevents the end of the sewing from unravelling. Figure 9.22 shows a hem sewn by this type of machine.

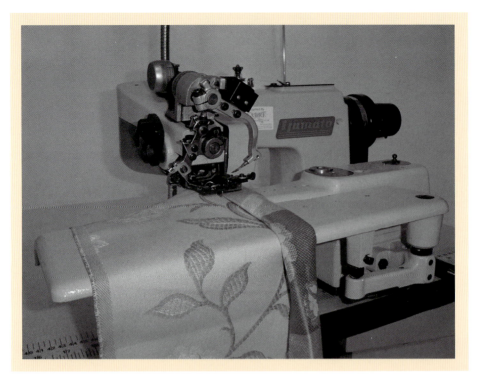

Figure 9.22.

Single-thread Button Sewing Machine (Figure 9.23): The machine shown has an electronically controlled system which automatically feeds correctly positioned buttons directly from the button hopper on the right into the button clamp. It is easily adjusted for sewing two or four hole buttons, and changing the number of stitches, say from 10 to 20, simply requires pressing a knob on the front of the machine. A special version of this machine has a needle penetration control whereby just two of the total stitches sewn are visible on the facing whilst the others are sewn through the forepart and fusible only.

Blind Spot-tacker (Figure 9.24): These machines are designed for sewing components hidden within side garments and an example of these would be the shoulder pads inside a ladies jacket.

Semi-automatic Machines

These are machines that are capable of doing one set of operations on the same garment; examples of these are shown in Figures 9.24 to 9.28.

These machines employ state of the art equipment enabling computerised technology to programme, for example, the number of buttonholes on a garment. Also to produce consistent and accurate sewing on many types of products, for instance the precise sewing of pockets on a pair of jeans. Embroidery machines are good examples of stitching techniques. Each embroidered

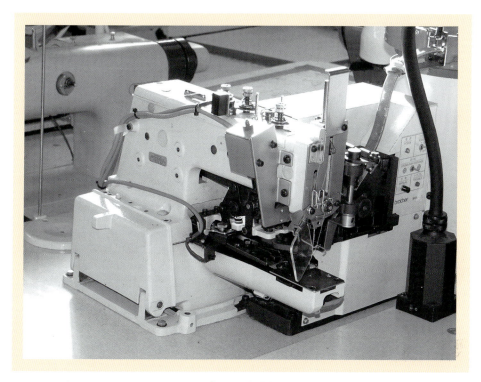

Figure 9.23.

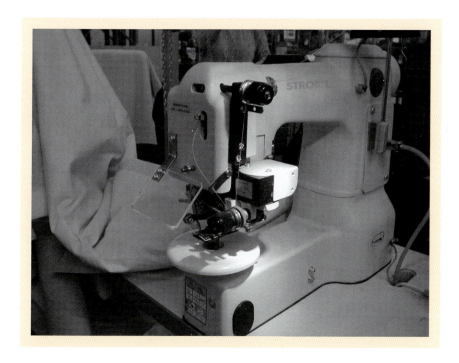

Figure 9.24.

Profile stitching (Figure 9.25)

Figure 9.25.

Pocket setting machine (Figure 9.26)

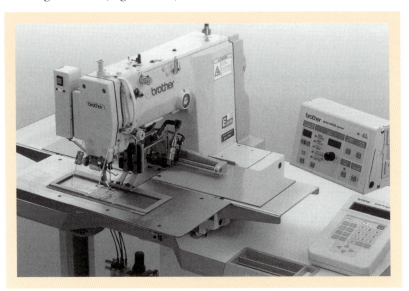

Figure 9.26.

Long seaming operations, trousers, curtains (Figure 9.27)

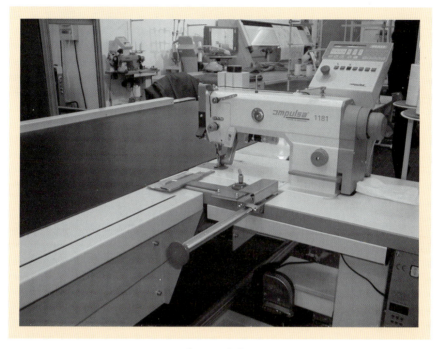

Figure 9.27.

design has been developed to be accurate and defined, to the point where technology has advanced to a stage that allows the minutest detail of a motif or graphic to be produced.

Embroidery machines (Figure 9.28)

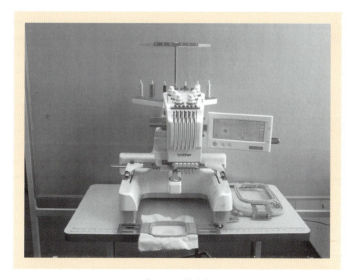

Figure 9.28.

CHAPTER 10

The Principles of Pressing Technology

Pressing can be defined as a process which changes the geometric fibre structure of the area being pressed by the controlled application of heat, steam and pressure. In this sense, removing a crease from a garment involves the same change of fibre lay as that required to open a seam or to press a hem.

With very few exceptions, every type of product manufactured by the clothing industry is pressed both during and at the end of its assembly, or at the end only. The exceptions are items of corsetry and underwear which, due to the materials and construction, do not require any form of pressing. At the other extreme from these "non-pressed" garments, the pressing operations required for a man's constructed jacket can account for about 25% of the total production time for the jacket. Regardless of the extent of pressing which garments undergo, pressing is a crucial process which imparts the final finish to a garment. A garment always has greater hanger or package appeal if it is appropriately pressed and finished.

CLASSIFICATIONS OF PRESSING

The total process of pressing can be divided into two groups of operations: under pressing and final pressing.

Under Pressing

This term covers all of the pressing operations performed on garments during their assembly. Seam opening, dart pressing and the pressing of flaps and patches are typical operations within this group.

Under pressing, when broken down into a sequence of operations, not only makes successive operations a little easier, but also enhances garment quality. For example, it is far easier for an operator to press a panelled back well if the component is on its own rather than closed to the shoulders and side seams of the fronts. This example demonstrates a good working principle for under pressing: when possible, the component should be positioned naturally during pressing and should not be constricted by other parts.

Final Pressing

Sometimes referred to as top pressing or off-pressing, this group includes all the operations used to finish garments when they have been completely assembled. The operations involved can range from a simple smoothing out with a hand iron to about fifteen machine and hand operations which are required to top press a woman's lined coat. The extent of the operations is determined by the construction of the garment, the fabric and, in some cases, how well the garment has been under pressed during its production.

There is no doubt that final pressing is the major process for finishing a garment and giving it its final appearance, but final pressing can only achieve the best results when performed on well made-up garments. Final pressing a badly constructed garment might help to ameliorate some of the faults, but it will never make a good garment out of what is basically a bad garment.

THE COMPONENTS OF PRESSING

Regardless of fabric, type of garment or the machinery and equipment employed, the majority of pressing operations have the same components (Figure 10.1).

Steam

The purpose of using pressurised steam is to relax the fibre structure of the fabric and make it pliable enough to be moulded by manipulation and pressure. Steam itself is an odourless, invisible gas consisting of vaporised water, and its white cloudy appearance is caused by minute water droplets interspersed in the vapour.

In factories, steam is generated by boilers fired by electricity or fossil fuels such as coal, gas or oil. Depending on the number of pressing work stations in the factory, steam can be distributed from a central boiler room or by small boilers located close to the work station. There are also independent pressing units which have a built-in boiler for generating their own steam.

Steam is a flexible, adaptable and efficient component of pressing. Some of its outstanding features are:

- It has a very high heat content.
- Its heat is generated at a constant temperature.
- It can be easily distributed and controlled.
- Water is relatively cheap and plentiful.

Steam has been used throughout the centuries for pressing and it is still the best medium for this purpose.

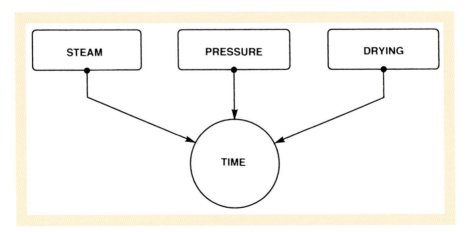

Figure 10.1.

Pressure

After steaming, manual or mechanical pressure is used to change the geometric fibre lay of the area being pressed. A simple example of this change is the pressing open of a regular seam. Figure 10.2A shows the fibre geometry of the cloth after the seam has been sewn and all the fibres are laying in one plane. After softening the fibre formation by steam and the application of pressure, each side of the seam has been folded back through 180° to lay flat on the component (Figure 10.2B). This structural change is typical of the majority of pressing operations.

Drying

Following the applications of steam and pressure, the area which has undergone these processes has to be dried and cooled in order that the fabric can revert to its natural moisture content and stable condition. The drying process is usually performed by a central vacuum pump which is connected to the pressing units, or by pumps built into the machine itself. The vacuum action removes the residual moisture from the material while it is lying on the pressing area.

Time

The length of time during which a component or garment is subjected to steaming, pressure and drying is a combined function of steam temperature, garment construction and the physical properties of the fabric being pressed. Whilst there are no fixed rules for the duration of these components, experimental trials utilising the appropriate fabric should be conducted prior to production.

Accurate control of the four components of pressing is essential to the maintenance of uniform quality. This is one of the main reasons why pressing machines can be programmed for the duration, operating conditions and sequence of all of the elements within a specific pressing operation.

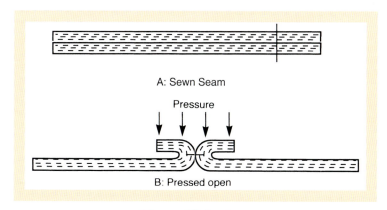

Figure 10.2A & B.

MACHINERY AND EQUIPMENT

The first mechanically operated pressing machine was introduced in 1905, and for the next 70 years or so many advances were made in constructing specialised machines and improving their methods of operation. Despite that, the pressing department remained relatively underdeveloped in clothing factories and it is only since the early 1980s that pressing has become a high-tech operation. For many years pressing machines were built around the traditional tailoring methods of pressing, but with the advent of synthetic materials, fusible interlinings and more scientific pattern making systems, pressing gradually became "engineered" rather than an imprecise copy of manual operations. The major lines of development are described here.

Programming

To reduce the reliance on skilled operators, various mechanical and electrical programming devices were developed which enabled the sequence and duration of the elements within an operation to be planned in advance. These systems required the operator simply to position the garment correctly on the machine with the aid of spotlight projectors which aligned with selected seams, and then to actuate the programme. In the 1990s microprocessors came into wider use and these enable the programming of operations for the pressing of different types of materials. The memory of the microprocessor holds these programs and the operator selects the one appropriate to the material to be pressed. This approach is very much in line with the developments in sewing machinery which reduce the skill input required from the operator and thus ensure the standard performance of an operation, together with consistent quality.

Combinations

Handling was always a large element in the time involved during and between pressing operations; when the "one machine, one operation" approach was dominant; the garment had to be handled constantly. Today the trend is to combine a series of contiguous operations into one machine thus eliminating the handling between the different operations performed by the machine. For example, the top pressing of the shoulder, sleeve head and armhole once required three separate machines. These three operations have been combined into one machine, with a significant reduction of handling time. Whilst individual specialised machines are still needed, the continuing development of combination machines has a high priority for the manufacturers of pressing machinery.

Waiting Time

Conventionally the operator loaded the programmed machine, actuated the program, waited until it was finished and then unloaded the machine. Obviously the operator's waiting time was non-productive time (and relatively expensive in high labour cost countries). The first attempt to reduce this wasteful factor was by arranging what are called tandem work stations (Figure 10.3). This consisted of

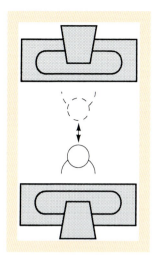

Figure 10.3.

two machines positioned opposite each other, with the machines able to perform the same or consecutive operations. The idea was that instead of the operator waiting for the completion of an operation, the machines would be operated alternately thus reducing waiting time.

This approach gradually led to the development of carousel machines which, in principle, operated as shown with this example relating to the under or top pressing of the left and right foreparts of a coat or jacket (Figure 10.4).

The circular plate of the machine holds two pairs of the lower bucks with a pair of top bucks supported on the back frame.

The operator loads one pair of fronts on the free lower bucks and then actuates the circular plate. This action turns the loaded bucks through 180° to the

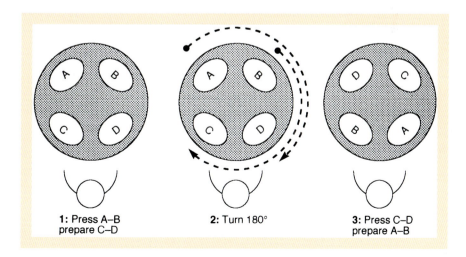

Figure 10.4.

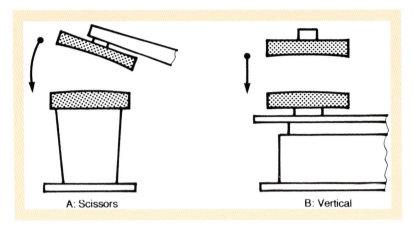

Figure 10.5.

back of the machine and simultaneously brings the pair of bucks from the back to face the operator.

Whilst the pair of fronts is being pressed at the back of the machine, the operator is able to unload the returned bucks and reload them ready for the next cycle.

Carousel type machines have two other advantages over conventional pressing machines:

(1) As all the pressing is carried out at the back of the machine, the operator is not continually working in a hot and steamy atmosphere.
(2) The vertical action of the top bucks provides more accurate alignment and pressure distribution between the top and bottom bucks than with the action of a regular scissor action machine (Figure 10.5).

Flexibility

Traditionally most under pressing operations were performed on a flat table, with or without the help of a sleeve board. The operator had to press every shape and form with this limited equipment and this required a great deal of skill in order to prevent the possible distortion of components. In addition, very few of these work stations had vacuum actions which meant that the operator had to let the hand iron dwell on the work in order to dry it. Under pressing units (Figure 10.6) are now fitted with two or three swivel arms, each of which supports a small buck that is designed for a specific purpose. The majority of these work stations have a vacuum action connected to the table and the bucks, and some have a warm compressed air system which generates a slight air cushion between the pressing area and the component.

This air cushion prevents direct contact between the buck and the work, thus reducing the possibility of shine on the pressed area.

Today the pressing department of a clothing factory has a technological level equal to that of most of the other production departments. The application of high-tech systems to pressing makes possible the optimum combination of quality and quantity.

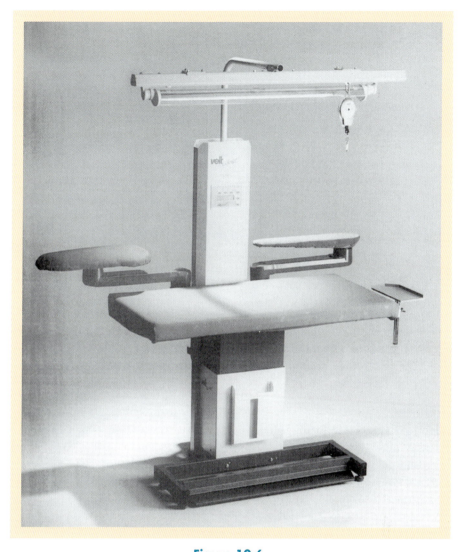

Figure 10.6.

Types of Machinery and Equipment

Sample rooms are rarely equipped with all the machinery and equipment required to completely press sample garments. It is possible to press samples of light clothing, such as dresses, blouses and nightdresses, on a versatile unit equipped with a hand iron. However, if the samples are of tailored garments, while most of the simple under pressing operations can be performed with a hand iron, there are still several operations which require the specialised machines in the factory. This is especially relevant to top pressing where most of the operations are performed on special purpose machines. The usual procedure was for the sample room to do what can be done correctly and then use the factory's machines for everything else. But now this is often not feasible due to the distance between design/product development and production facilities.

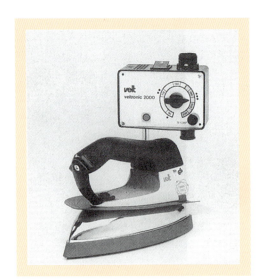

Figure 10.7.

There are many different types of pressing machines on the market because of the variety of garment types produced, each with its own specific pressing requirements. The rest of this section will examine some of the items which are representative of their type.

Hand Irons

Figure 10.7 shows a typical electric high-pressure steam iron which is used for numerous operations in the production of clothing. The iron illustrated weighs 1.5 kg and the separate temperature control has an accuracy of +/-28°C.

Hand irons are produced in a variety of shapes and weights to suit specific types of operation (Figure 10.8).

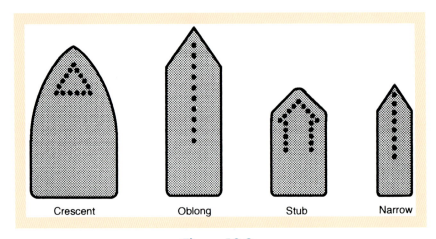

Crescent   Oblong   Stub   Narrow

Figure 10.8.

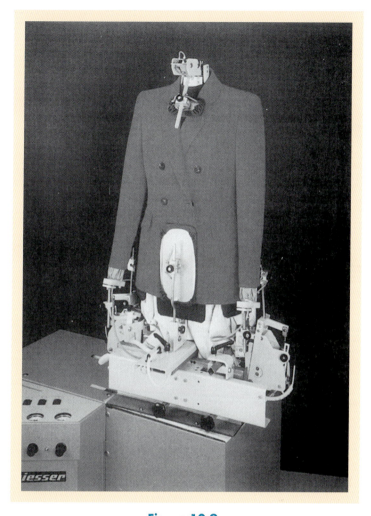

Figure 10.9.

Form Finishing Machines

The form finishing machine in Figure 10.9 is one of the types used for finishing men's and women's jackets and skirts. During the pressing operation the body and sleeves are precisely tensioned by pneumatically operated clamps or pressure pads which can be set for individual forms. A microprocessor monitors and regulates the programmed times, temperatures and the sequence or combination of steam, hot air, cold air and vacuum.

Cabinet Presses

The small cabinet press shown in Figure 10.10 is designed to press and heatset shirts before they are buttoned, thus preventing button marks on the finished article. During the pressing process the back and front are tensioned by air-filled bags, which ensure an even pressing surface when the shirt is between the two shaped pressing

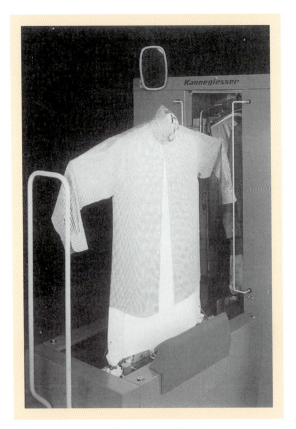

Figure 10.10.

Figure 10.11.

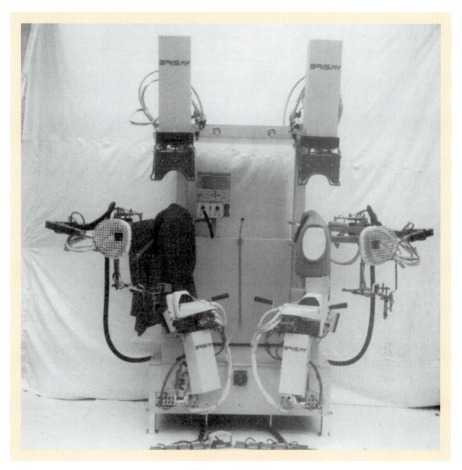

Figure 10.12.

plates. This particular machine can be efficiently operated by one person only when there is a reasonable balance between the handling and pressing cycle times.

The unit illustrated in Figure 10.11 is a tunnel finisher for knitwear which can carry up to 30 articles at a time through the finishing processes. The tunnel has two sections, one for gentle steaming and the other for quick drying of the garment. Garment forms can be adjusted for different styling and sizes and the microprocessor controls the processing time, steaming time and the quantity and steam and air temperatures. Up to 24 individual pressing programs can be stored in the microprocessor.

Combination Pressing Machines

A high-tech pressing machine for men's and women's clothing is illustrated in Figure 10.12. This machine has a digital programmer and presses the shoulder, sleeve head and sleeve cuff in one set-up.

CHAPTER 11

Garment Finishing and Inspection

Finishing and inspection are the last two major operations in the manufacture of garments before they are bagged or boxed and delivered to the finished goods warehouse. In most factories these two operations are performed by separate departments.

All sample garments also have to be finished and inspected and this is done in the sample room for convenience and because of the close involvement of the designer at each stage. These two processes are vital in the production of sample garments because finishing ensures that the garment is correctly completed in every detail, and inspection verifies that it conforms to the relevant quality standards. In addition, this is the stage when the designer makes the final assessment of whether the sample garment has achieved its planned design objectives and can be approved.

During the finishing and inspection of samples, nothing which concerns the garment technically can be left to chance. Once orders have been taken and production commenced, it could be very expensive for the factory to deal with quality or manufacturing problems which should have been detected and rectified in the sample room.

FINISHING

As the name implies, finishing covers all the operations required to complete a garment. For most garments this process starts after top pressing. The details involved in finishing vary according to garment type but in principle are as described here.

Attaching Buttons

Attaching buttons has two stages, marking and sewing.

Marking

The hand marking of button positions requires accuracy in four respects:

(1) For symmetrical garments the button positions have to ensure the overall symmetry of the garment. Some of the important points to observe are:
   • Collar ends and lapel steps on both fronts must be the same distance down from the neck line.
   • Pockets have to be at the same height.
   • Lateral seams need to be matched across the fronts.
   • Darts should start and finish at the same levels.
(2) The button spacings have to be exact in order to ensure flat laying fronts
(3) The specified wrap allowance must be observed
(4) With striped or checked materials, pattern symmetry and alignment are essential.

Sewing

The buttons of classic shirt and blouse samples are generally sewn on during production by automatic button sewers. These machines can be set for specific spacings and the buttons are automatically fed to the button clamp. As factories producing these types of garments mostly work to standard spacings, sewing the buttons on to the occasional sample does not interfere too much with production.

The buttoning of garments when they have been completed is usually performed in the sample room as this is more convenient than using the button sewing machines in the factory. Buttons should not be sewn onto garments which will be subjected to pressure during their top pressing. Apart from leaving an impression of the button on the cloth, there is also every possibility that the button could be broken by the pressure of the pressing machine bucks. Knitted and other garments which are steam finished only can be safely buttoned before top pressing.

Labels

Labels are of great benefit for the wearer, and an important aspect of finishing sample garments is to ensure that the correct labels are in the right positions. Some labels are attached during the production of the sample, whilst others are sewn on when the garment is being finished. Most companies have a standard specification for the types and positions of labels on their garments.

There are legal requirements for some types of garment labels, such as:

- Flammability of materials used for children's nightwear.
- Fibre content, for example 35% cotton – 65% polyester.
- Garments produced for export have to carry a "country of origin" label. This is usually inserted on the brand label.
- Although there are no legal directives at the time of writing concerning the following labels, most clothing manufacturers use them to provide guidance for the consumer:

  Care labels – These provide very specific information regarding washing and ironing temperatures, whether or not bleaching agents can be used, and the suitable types of dry cleaning solvents.

  Size labels – These have to be suitable to the country or countries where the garment is to be sold. It is pointless to export garments carrying British or EU sizing system labels to a country using a totally different sizing nomenclature. Whenever possible, the size labels should be positioned so as to be immediately visible and not necessitate a search on the part of the prospective purchaser.

Irrespective of the number and types of labels used for a garment, they should:

- Be of an acceptable size.
- Maintain their legibility after repeated washing or dry cleaning during the normal life of the garment.
- Be securely affixed to the garment. It does not do much for the quality image of a garment if labels flap around loosely or fall off after a short period of wear.
- Be easily seen by the consumer and not hidden away in awkward places.

In factories labels are attached by a variety of machines, ranging from the regular sewing machine to microprocessor controlled machines which hold the memories required to attach different sized labels. Some of these machines also have an automatic label feed and positioning system which only requires the operator to position the component or garment correctly.

Cleaning

The last stage of the finishing process is to thoroughly clean the garment of all thread ends and stains. This means that the sample has to be inspected very carefully because nothing gives a worse impression to a buyer than trailing threads or un-removed stains on the inside or outside of the garment.

Final Touches

Sample garments often require some hand finishing with steam. A very effective tool for this is the stand-mounted iron shown in Figure 11.1. The height and angle of the iron can be adjusted in order to operate it in a static position, or it can be removed and used by hand. A steam brush can be fitted to the iron sole when it is used to remove shine and marks from velour, velvet and other napped cloths.

When the sample garment has been checked for finish it is ready for the final phase of its manufacture inspection before it leaves the sample room.

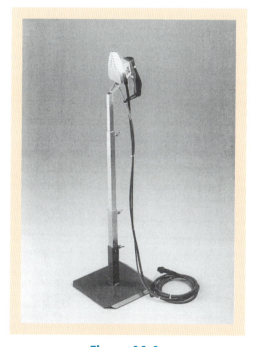

Figure 11.1.

INSPECTION

Inspection is crucial for sample garments because apart from design considerations, there are a number of important factors involved. This is the moment when the sample receives the go or no-go signal and this decision requires some practical considerations on the part of the designer. The principal factors involved are given here.

Fitting Quality

There are two basic approaches to fitting quality. The one used may be company policy or may be based more on custom and usage, and this dictates how the sample room has to work. The two approaches are live models and workroom stands:

Live Models

A live fit model is used to both display the garment to the development team, and or the buyer, as well as to allow an evaluation of fit. The model used will be of an average size within the brand's size chart (say a 12) and taking into account shape variation within sizes will give a transferable evaluation of garment fit.

Workroom Stands

Modern workroom stands are constructed according to the results of scientific anthropometric surveys and they embody an accurate combination of the figuration and measurements of a specific population group. In effect the workroom stand mirrors the targeted potential consumer who generally has different physical characteristics from those of a professional catwalk model. For practical and commercial purposes, the workroom stand is the principal criterion for measurements and basic fitting.

There seems to be an obvious answer to the dilemma of live models or workroom stands. Why not use models having the same or very similar measurements to those of the stands used for samples? Unfortunately this is difficult to achieve because the nature of their profession demands that models should have a close resemblance to the concept of an ideal form. This concept is more than somewhat divorced from the realities of commercial sizing.

There is a practical solution to the problem of judging the fitting quality of samples. Sample garments should be made from production patterns for the workroom stand and then checked for ease of movement and fitting quality on the model. This approach does not rule out the possibility of some minor alteration to the sample in order to enhance its appearance on the model. This is of particular significance because changing the measurements and fitting of a model-based pattern to a production pattern can lead to a host of new technical problems which no one really needs.

Measurements

An integral part of the inspection of samples is the checking of finished measurements. Whilst measurements do not fully indicate fitting quality, checking is necessary especially if the garment has to conform to a customer's measurement specification.

The checking of garment measurements has to take into account the question of reasonable tolerances which do not have a noticeable influence on the fitting, design and functionality of the garment. Tolerances can be defined as the allowable deviations from standards, and in practical terms this requires a sense of proportion. The deviation of 0.5 cm in the length of a dress which should be 100 cm long is not the same as a deviation of 0.5 cm in the length of a shoulder having an intended length of 12.5 cm. Therefore every deviation should be considered in relation to the planned length or size of the part being measured.

Viewing the Garment

The most effective method of viewing a sample garment to inspect its detailed and general appearance is to look at it in the same way as the consumer does in a shop, but with a professional eye. This means that the shop situation should be duplicated in the sample room and requires a very simple arrangement.

A full length cheval mirror should be positioned close to a convenient wall, with a workroom stand facing it at a distance of 1.20 m to 1.50 m. The inspector needs to stand behind the stand, look over its shoulder and view the garment in the mirror (Figure 11.2). The recommended routine is to view the garment in four consecutive stages, revolving the stand through 90° after completing each stage. Start with the front view, follow with the first side view, then the back, and finish with the second side. When viewing, the eyes should move in a tight zigzag pattern from side to side, starting at the neckline and gradually working down to the hem. Good lighting is essential and by using this method very little will escape the eye of an alert inspector.

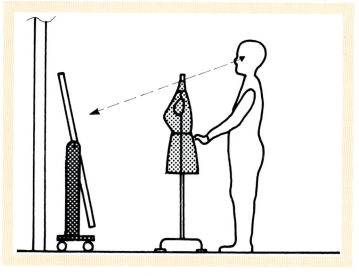

Figure 11.2.

In addition to inspecting the external appearance of a sample, it is no less important to inspect the internal appearance. This inspection is necessary for all types of garments because sewing faults or other errors are easily seen on unlined garments, and stains or damages are very noticeable on linings. Today consumers have increasing demands for garment quality, and inspecting the internal and external appearance of a garment is an integral part of the quality chain which fundamentally starts in the sample room.

Quality Standards

The inspection of a sample garment has to be relevant to its price and target market. There is no practical reason to apply stringent quality standards to samples which, if mass produced, will only undergo the most rudimentary of inspection procedures. It is often said that a thing should be done only as well as it needs to be done, and this is very true of clothing. There is no one universal quality standard for all garments, but rather each category of garment has its own quality criteria. After all, there is a significant difference between the acceptable quality of a garment bought off a stall in a street market and that of a garment purchased from a reputable store.

However, both these retail outlets purchase merchandise from clothing manufacturers and every manufacturer attempts to cater, as best they can, for a specific market sector. Clothing producers of all types require buyers and it is the bottom line of the balance sheet which counts in business and not necessarily citations for quality.

WORKING METHODS

This section could also be entitled "the follow-up" because in most factories sampling does not end with the production of sample garments. Checking samples has far broader implications.

Some factories employ the "sealed-sample" system whereby a sample garment is given the seal of approval and marked accordingly. It is then used by the production unit as the standard for quality and production. There are some operations, such as top pressing, which are difficult to define in a garment quality specification and it is far more practical and effective to use a garment to demonstrate what is required, rather than to rely on words. In this instance one picture really is worth a thousand words.

A widely used method of checking the quality and production viability of a sample is to produce a pilot-run under factory conditions. Usually the number of garments in a pilot-run is that which can be cut from one roll of cloth, but each company has its own ideas of what is necessary as regards quantity. Pilot-run garments are closely followed up during their production and the feedback to the designer and pattern cutter is almost immediate. Some of the larger retail organisations request grading trials in order to check the sizing of the garments on order, and often the grading trials are used by the factory as pilot-runs.

One thing is certain: garment quality should never be left to chance and the combination of exacting inspection procedures for samples and the feedback from pilot-runs goes a long way towards eliminating any chance elements.

AQL (Acceptable Quality Limit) Procedure

The quality focus should be upon PREVENTION not DETECTION and companies have developed procedures The AQL Audit consists of two sections which include:

- Finished stock.
- Measured checks.

It is essential that the quality of garments going into finished stock is monitored whilst the Finished Stock Audit provides a method of feedback from the customer's perspective; the AQL Audit is based on the Standard set before beginning production in bulk and is viewed from the garment and style technical specification.

The initial audit will be carried out with a specific team with follow-up audits being carried out internally. The scope of this procedure is normally exclusive to the manufacturing companies concerned.

Responsibilities and Reporting

The responsibility for the completion of the audit is usually divided between two teams as listed below.

Team 1	**Team 2**
Quality Assurance Manager	Factory Manager
Factory Manager	Garment Technologist
Garment Technologist	Quality Supervisor
Quality Supervisor	Line Supervisor

Line Supervisor

The relevant Technical Executive and the Production Manager may be present in either team. The audit will not take place without the presence of the Factory or Production Manager.

The initial audit will be carried out by Team 1 and any subsequent audits will be carried out by Team 2.

Factory Manager

The factory manager is responsible for ensuring that there is sufficient finished stock for the audit to take place. The minimum quantity of finished stock is 50 dozen (600 garments).

The factory manager is also responsible for ensuring that all subsequent audits are carried out, i.e. all colour/fabric options and follow-up audits in the event of garments failing to meet the required specification. The results should be formally communicated on the relevant documentation of the Quality Assurance Manager.

The sample rail should be accompanied by a copy of the AQL audit and all members of the team should have a copy.

Circulation List

- Managing Director.
- Factory Manager.
- Design Manager.
- Quality Assurance Supervisor.
- Garment Technologist.

AQL Procedure

- The factory manager will advise the Quality Assurance Manager that sufficient stock is available for the audit and agree a date for the audit to take place.
- The relevant team will select the required quantity of stock (minimum 80 garments) from the warehouse consisting of all available sizes.
- The audit will take place in a well lit area designated for this purpose.
- The garments will be compared against the accepted standard and any deviations from the standard will be classified either Major or Minor.
- Any deviations from the standard will be recorded on the form.

Measurements

- Two garments of each size will be measured for critical measurements.
- The variance (+/−) from the specified measurement should be recorded with any measurements outside the tolerance circled.

NOTE: Each measurement which is out of tolerance is a major defect

Documentation

- All sections of the form must be completed.
- In the event of the garments failing to meet the required specification, the reverse side of the form will be completed by the factory manager.
- The subsequent audit will be recorded on the lower section of the reverse side of the form.

The completed forms will be filed in the proper manner in a secure location with access by the Quality Assurance Manager or the factory manager. An example of the form is given in Figure 11.3 below:

FOR COMPLETION BY THE FACTORY MANAGER

FACTORY _____ **STROKE NO** _____ **DEPT** _____ **COLOUR**

	QTY IN STOCK	QTY DEFECTIVE	% DEFECTIVE	DEFECTS	
				MAJOR	MINOR
FACTORY				% MINOR DEFECTS	
WAREHOUSE					
TOTAL					
ACTION TAKEN TO PREVENT RECURRENCE					

2nd AQL AUDIT

BATCH QTY	MAJOR		MINOR		THREAD ENDS (QTY)		
	QTY	%	QTY	%	MEASUREMENTS (CM)		
					AREA	QTL	
SAMPLE SIZE							
MAX DEFECTS							
AUDIT TEAM							
					PASS / FAIL		
					NEXT AUDIT DATE		
					FACTORY	MGR	SIG

COMMENTS / ACTION   CIRCULATION

Figure 11.3.

CHAPTER 12

Selecting
Appropriate Technology

It should be evident from the preceding sections that the level of technology employed in the design and production of fashion products is extensive and can represent a sizable investment for any company. If a design requires the acquisition of a new piece of technology it is imperative to make an appropriate selection to avoid unnecessary expenditure, limit the negative impact on existing systems and efficiently enable the production of the new design.

It is important to remember that technological change concerns all things new to any organisation, be that equipment or systems.

The overall process of selecting and implementing new technology can be considered as a 4 phase model.

(1) Initiation – The stimulus for change, the reason for change – to be able to produce a new design.
(2) Planning – The essential intermediate phase which reduces uncertainties, governs the efficiency of the project and helps understand the aims of the project.
(3) Application – Making the project happen, turning the plan into activity.
(4) Consolidation – Bringing the project online and planning the continued use of the technology as a lifetime asset.

Based on suitable sources of information it is important to apply a systematic approach to quantifying the responses. A basic starting point is to employ a Kepner-Tregoe matrix (Table 12.1A) technique to marshal the information.

Table 12.1A.

Factor/Question	Option 1	Option 2	Option 3	Option 4
A	6	5	3	1
B	10	4	10	2
C	3	10	9	8
D	1	5	6	3
E	1	10	10	10
F	3	3	3	2
	24	**37**	**41**	**26**

Options 1 and 4 would probably be eliminated; the decision between options 2 and 3 may be made on financial grounds.

But not all of these factors would be as important to the application of the technology, for example aesthetics may be less important than reliability. To account for this, the selection team can prioritise the attributes being satisfied (Table 12.1B).

Table 12.1B.

		Option							
		1	**1w**	**2**	**2w**	**3**	**3w**	**4**	**4w**
Factor	**Weight**								
A	1	6	6	5	5	3	3	1	1
B	3	10	30	4	12	10	30	2	6
C	2	3	6	10	20	9	18	8	16
D	1	1	1	5	5	6	6	3	3
E	1	1	1	10	10	10	10	10	10
F	1	3	3	3	3	3	3	2	2
		24	**47**	37	**55**	41	**70**	26	**38**

W = Weighted score, clearly option 3(w) now has the advantage.

A radar diagram can be used to illustrate this information much more effec-tively for communication purposes. Each "arm" of the graph is an attribute or factor, the weighted score is plotted along this arm and the points connected. Using a different colour for each option allows the viewer to appreciate that the one approaching the full circle in area is the most suitable technology.

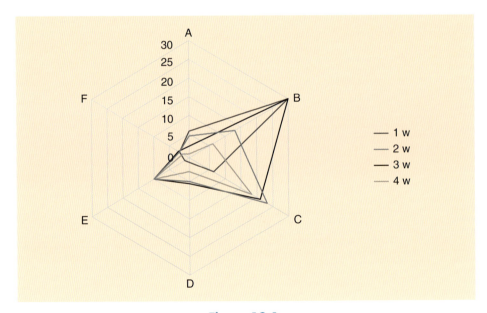

Figure 12.1.

CAPITAL INVESTMENT APPRAISAL (CIA)

In order to conduct any kind of CIA you need to take a look at aspects of –ve and +ve cash flows as a result of capital investment in new technologies.

Basic Types

Easy payback period:	$\dfrac{\text{initial capital investment}}{\text{annual +ve cash flow (savings)}}$

Discounted Cash Flow (Net Present Value and Internal Rate of Return): rely on the time value of money (almost the opposite case to the money being invested in a savings account).

If you filter through all of the techniques available for capital investment appraisal, when applied in the clothing and textile industry, two things become apparent:

- Insufficient benefits analysis.
- The setting of high "hurdle rates".

Areas of potential benefit that are often under appreciated include:

Tangible
- Reduced maintenance bills.
- Resale value of existing technology.
- Government grant aid for investment.
- Reduced raw materials consumption.
- Reduced energy consumption.
- Space savings.
- Reduced labour costs.

Intangible/less tangible
- Improved quality
  Reduced "RTM" (rework)
  Increased sales through reputation.
- Increased manufacturing flexibility
  Increased market share
  Reduced set-up/change over time=cost.
- Improved market standing.
- Reduced stock
  Lower working capital in raw materials/WIP
  Reduced property expenditure through reduced storage.

These less tangible benefits are the hardest to use in justifying investment in new technologies. They are less open to rigorous and quantifiable assessment and excluded by the short term financial appraisal techniques. However, many of these benefits give rise to a strategic advantage and are becoming the main indicators for successful adoption of AMT/S.

Because the benefits from investment are difficult to estimate a situation arises where new technologies are subjected to asymmetric assessment. The main problem is that the investment costs are known and the benefits are estimated.

Taking a closer look at investment costs:

- Purchase costs.
- Installation costs
  Removal of existing "tech"
  Space preparation
  Services
  Safety.
- Training costs.
- Project costs.
- Maintenance costs.

One can appreciate that these are "hard" figures, easily predicted and quantified.

Having defined through projection and quantification financial investment in the new technology and return from that investment (to a greater or lesser accuracy) by estimation, the application of high hurdle rates is another limiting factor on the implementation of new technologies in the fashion business.

High Hurdle Rates

It is common within the sewn products industry to expect a payback period of two to three years or less, or to apply a "cost of capital" value of 20–30% in DCF methods (NPV and IRR respectively).

These levels favour short term projects at the exclusion of projects which would generate increased returns in the later stages of their use/life.

Combined with the insufficient benefits analysis the high hurdle rates produce a double penalty when considering capital investment. The ability to see beyond these measures and make an entrepreneurial assessment could be the difference between the success and failure of an organisation to realise a new design – take the risk.

PART 3

THE OPERATION OF THE PRODUCT DEVELOPMENT DEPARTMENT

CHAPTER 13

The Sample Room

The sample garment may be required for several purposes and may not need to be of the same specification in each application. A design sample may only need to demonstrate the concept of the product, a fit sample need only be of the correct size and shape and a production sample should be made in exactly the way it would be made in full production. So why won't one sample do all these things? If you design in Western Europe and commission a sale there but manufacture in East Asia it is likely that you would not have full access to all manufacturing technologies near the design room. If you need to do a fit session with a UK buyer then you may need to make and adjust a sample garment near to that organisation and far away from the production site.

In factories, production units work on bulk and according to pre-planned production processes and inspection routines. Production operators specialise in relatively small operations, with nearly every operation performed on a machine or item of equipment constructed expressly for the purpose. The work flow is balanced and, all things being equal, these factory units operate with a consistent rhythm. In its own way the sample room also manufactures clothing but its production is strongly characterised by the intermittent nature of its working. Every new sample garment presents a new combination of design and technical problems and solutions have to be found whilst the garment is in production.

Whilst sample production contains a large number of standard operations, new operations are continually being developed and sometimes these necessitate a considerable amount of trial and error work. New types of fabrics are frequently being tried out and their reactions to fusing, sewing and pressing have to be closely observed and modifications made when called for. Fashion designers and pattern cutters are not omnipotent and often changes are made to the original design during a sample garment's production. These changes nearly always require new or adjusted patterns and possibly the revision of the original materials usage quantities. In addition, the designer could ask to see a sample garment at various stages in order to check if certain ideas are working, whether a new fabric is proving to be suitable, etc.

Producing samples is a sporadic operation which requires close and active direction by management in order to achieve the planned objectives.

OPERATIONAL CONDITIONS

Unlike a regular production unit which works within a uniform structure, the sample room operates under different conditions for the following reasons.

In the majority of sample rooms the standard unit of production is a single garment. Some companies also produce in the sample room the copy samples required for agents and representatives, although this is rather a misuse of highly skilled labour.

Every new sample garment is unique by virtue of its design and/or fabric. As a sample it is a one-off garment which is only brought to life in the sample room and when completed and approved, it is handed over to the marketing department.

The sample room is not generally equipped with all the same types of specialised machines as those in the factory. Consequently, when necessary, some operations required for samples have to be performed outside the sample room. At times this means that sample garments have to wait until a production operator is free to carry out the work. This is yet another small factor which contributes to the intermittent nature of sample room production.

As the sample room staff have to produce constantly changing products, their versatility, adaptability and quality is, in most cases, more important than their speed. They are not specialists in the same sense as production operators because they are specialists in making samples and not in performing a few short operations at a high rate. Therefore, whilst time is an important factor in relation to sample production, it has to be on a far looser scale than the time standards used by the factory.

The operating conditions of the sample room are in sharp contrast to those prevailing in the factory, although both units are concerned with producing garments. Hence it follows that there must also be a considerable difference between their production methods.

PRODUCTION METHODS

If anything is the key to the production methods used in the sample room it is the scale of operation. The production of two or three samples daily is totally different from producing, say, 20 or 30 samples per day. This is not just a numerical difference which can be dealt with by more people, machinery and space, but it demands a completely different approach to the concept of sample production. The following two examples examine the major disparities between the small and large scale production of samples.

Small Scale

In a small scale set-up, apart from a sample cutter there might only be three or four operators. The production method most often used in this situation is called "making-through". As its name suggests, an individual operator performs nearly every operation required to make a sample. A typical unit could have one operator doing all the special machine operations, such as overlocking, blindstitching and buttonholes, as well as helping out with other work when needed. The other operators would concentrate on sewing, handwork and pressing, plus whatever else was necessary to complete the garment. The layout of this type of sample room has to be convenient for the operators but no more than that, because basically only one operator controls the work flow of a garment.

This production method requires highly skilled and versatile personnel and although it is somewhat expensive, it is a practical and effective way of producing small numbers of samples.

Large Scale

In a sample room producing a large number of samples every day, the production method would lean towards that used by a small and well-organised factory production unit. The work would be broken down into groups of related operations, with operators mainly specialising in one group only. These groups could be:

- Special machine operations.
- All types of sewing.
- Under pressing.
- Finishing.
- Top pressing.
- Inspection, etc.

The layout would be planned so that garments advance progressively from group to group without the need for constant back-tracking on the part of the operators. Whilst this production method also relies to a large extent on the versatility of its personnel, the operators are able to develop specialist group skills instead of being jacks of all trades.

Factory Produced Samples

The previous two examples of production methods include a limited reliance on the facilities of the factory to carry out operations for which the sample room lacks the necessary specialised machinery or equipment. The construction of some types of garments, such as women's corsetry, requires an extensive range of specialised machinery and it is not viable to equip the sample room with this.

In this situation the sample room would cut the sample and then a member of the staff would accompany and guide it through the factory, from process to process. When the sample had completed its tour of the factory, the sample room would then attend to the finishing and inspection details. This method of producing samples is not particularly convenient but is a practical alternative to equipping another small factory in the sample room.

PERSONNEL AND RESPONSIBILITIES

As mentioned previously, the sample room staff have to possess the professional attributes needed for the production of samples. Every operator has a definite area of responsibility regarding their own work and that of their co-workers. Sample garments do not have ready prepared detailed specifications because specifications are derived from approved samples and not the other way round. As a result, the specification is gradually built up in the sample room and as it is practically impossible to continually watch over every operation, the personnel have to be relied upon to take full responsibility for what they are doing. What this means for different kinds of operator is explained here.

Cutters

Initially cutters have to verify that the requisite tests on materials have been carried out, and in the event of serious deviations they need to report them and obtain approval to cut the sample. Disregarding this elementary procedure could involve the company in the bulk purchase of unsuitable materials. Irrespective of whether the cutting markers are prepared locally or at a distance, the cutter has to be able to evaluate accurately a marker's efficiency – a critical area of cost saving is available here. He or she has to be sufficiently responsible to know when it is justified to call in the designer to examine possible pattern modifications which could improve material usage.

Sewing Machine Operators

Sewing machine operators have a wide range of responsibilities including the correct selection of needles and threads, determining the appropriate stitch length, verifying seam strength and checking on possible seam damage, especially when new materials are being tried out. The sewing machine operator also has to be a good judge of a pattern's accuracy and practicality and has a responsibility to inform the pattern cutter if there are any pattern related problems.

Special Machine Operators

Special machine operators have to know a great deal about many machines and be capable of making sound appraisals of the performance of each one on every fabric being worked on. Most competent special machine operators know how to adjust their various machines according to specific demands, but they also have to know when to request the assistance of a mechanic if the problem is beyond their know-how. Calling on a mechanic is more responsible behaviour than giving up and saying that the operation cannot be done. Adjustments required should be recorded in order to inform the production unit when setting up lines to cope with the new or changed product.

Pressers

The responsibilities of pressers extend to two main aspects:

(1) When incorrect work reaches them, they should be able to recognise faults and be sufficiently familiar with the operations in the sample room to know who to inform regarding the mistakes.
(2) Their practical evaluations of the reactions of a particular material to pressing can be critical to the decision to purchase the material.

Pressers do not only press the output of previous sewing or other operations but they are also contributing to the final appearance of the sample. They have to be aware of this responsibility and do far more than open seams or press hems.

Finishing

This group of operations also has responsibilities because operators working on finishing can often see small details that need correction before the sample is produced in bulk. It is relatively easy to cover up most of these small details by some additional handwork or by other means, but factories cannot afford this type of extraneous work. The finishing operative who has a sense of responsibility would point out these errors to the appropriate person.

Quality

There has to be an individual and joint responsibility on the part of the sample room staff regarding the quality of the garments which they produce. Every employee has to be fully acquainted with the required quality standards and be capable of making independent and objective judgements of the quality of their own work. They also have to help each other by pointing out quality errors to their co-workers. This is not a point-scoring situation but rather an honest acceptance of the collective responsibility for sample quality. Another worker may not be perfect, but then neither are you.

Training

Due to natural labour turnover there will always be a small group of learners in the sample room. An essential part of their initiation into work is to thoroughly acquaint them with the responsibilities which go with their particular job.

THE VIRTUAL SAMPLE

2-D to 3-D digital technologies are advancing to a stage where 3-D virtual garments can be created from the digital 2-D pattern pieces to a sufficient level that selection decisions from design concept can be made confidently based on this virtual sample. Garment fit can be visualised and assessed on 3-D avatars "wearing" the virtual sample – be that to the size of the retailer's standard fit model or the consumer's own specific measurements – but decisions come much less confidently. That said, it is still most common to have to produce a physical sample for a buyer to see and handle, a technologist to measure flat on their table and see move on a person. A good compromise between the two is the use of web based video technologies to communicate between production and design/technology. Thus a physical sample can be produced (relatively quickly) and worn/modelled to be evaluated by a team via web video remote from the production site. Of course the digital technologies will develop further and are much more important when making an initial decision to commission a product without having to purchase and use the physical components necessary to create a real garment – a move towards a sustainable digital product development approach.

CHAPTER 14

Communication

The communication of information is an integral part of the day-to-day working routine in the design department. In operational terms, these communications have three forms:

(1) The garment identification system used within the company.
(2) The means and the type of information by which the designer communicates with the design and sample room staff at the inception of the design.
(3) The form and content of the information which has to be communicated to other departments on the completion and handing over of the sample garment.

In all instances the accuracy of the information transmitted is important because there is no place for guesswork in an organisation which wants to be efficient.

GARMENT IDENTIFICATION

Nearly every person working for a clothing manufacturer is dealing with garments in one way or another, and communication between them is simplified if they all use the same terminology to define the products they are handling. One method of achieving a simple common language is to use working style numbers as the basic code of communication. An example of this follows.

Example

It is preferable to use a four figure working style number rather than a computer generated number which can run into seven or eight alphanumeric characters that are not easy to remember. Table 14.1A shows an example of a unique style numbering system. The significance of each of the four numbers is:

Table 14.1A.

Garment	No.	Season	Phase	No.	Consecutive No.
Skirts	1	Spring	1	1	1
Trousers	2	Spring	2	2	x
Dresses	3	Summer	1	3	x
Blouses	4	Autumn	1	4	x
Vests	5	Winter	1	5	x
Jackets	6	Winter	2	6	99

Table 14.1B.

Style 3526	3	5	26
	dress	Winter-phase 1	Consecutive No.

First number

This denotes the garment category, i.e.

1 = Skirts   2 = Trousers   3 = Dresses etc

Therefore the type of garment being dealt with is immediately recognisable by its first number.

Second number

Seasons are usually divided into phases and the seasons with their individual phases, recur every year. The objective of the second number is to introduce a time context for a garment so that people will know whether it belongs to the past, current or future season, and to what phase of that particular season. The central column of Table 14.1B shows how this aspect of the numbering system operates.

Third and fourth numbers

These refer to the consecutive numbers given to the successive garments developed in each garment category. The example system can accommodate 99 different garments in one category for one phase of a season.

DESIGNER TO OTHERS

Once the decision has been taken to develop a particular design, the design will remain only an idea unless it is translated into a garment. This means that the designer has to prepare a design specification which is a detailed and precise presentation of the planned design and technical objectives of the garment. This specification can have both formal and informal aspects because some details, such as materials, have definite references, whereas the description of a design feature can be in the shorthand language of the design department. For example, a material could have the number 4062, but a collar might be described as "about 2 cm wider all round than style 605". Some of the items which a design specification should contain are given here.

Working Sketch

This is sometimes called a technical flat and is intended as a pure working drawing and not as a fashion journal illustration. Apart from the regular front and back views, this sketch should also show any new or complex design features drawn to a legible scale. All the appropriate design information should be written on the sketch so that the pattern cutter and other members of the staff know exactly what is involved.

Size and Measurements

Although sample garments are generally all made in the same size, there can be exceptions, so the required sample size has to be recorded. Some customers request that samples should be made according to their size charts, in which case the relevant information has to be noted on the design specification. If the sample has any features which have special measurements, these too should be noted.

Special Processes

This refers to all processes which are not within the regular framework, such as pleating, embroidery and the use of special packaging. Everything which comes under this heading should be listed and, if necessary, accompanied by a small sample or sketch.

Fabrics

Cuttings of all the materials to be used should be attached to the specification and their complete details recorded. If there are any special comments regarding a particular material, these have to be noted.

In theory new materials should arrive at the sample room after undergoing the requisite tests, but where no formal procedures exist for testing sample lengths, the sample section has to do its own basic testing. In the main this concerns checking the reaction of top cloths to pressing and fusing. If anything more than an acceptable level of reaction occurs, the material should be carefully evaluated as to whether it can be used or needs to be rejected. Materials such as linings and fusible interlinings from suppliers with proven track records do not have to be tested prior to cutting each new sample, but an occasional test is a wise precaution.

Trimmings

Under this heading are details of all the other materials which have been selected for use on the sample. Among others these include buttons, press studs, pads, decorative tapes, zips, appliqués and special sewing threads.

The extent of this part of the design specification is dependent on the category of garment produced by the company. Specifying all the trimmings for a functional waterproof outer garment is considerably more extensive than for a school blouse. But whatever the variety of trimmings required for a sample garment, nothing should be omitted.

Labels

While this subject has been covered in a previous chapter, there are some additional points which are particularly relevant to sample garments, covering two aspects:

(1) Label type – The type and format of labels used by a company is usually standardised and for the design specification it is a question of selecting and

noting those which are applicable. Many labels are printed and if there are different requirements from the stock items, say for care labels, these have to be ordered. Brand labels are generally held in stock by the trimmings stores.

(2) Label positioning – Most companies have standard guidelines for the positioning of labels and any planned deviations from this standard have to be noted on the design specification.

Importance of the Specification

In a practical sense, the design specification is the primary planning and control tool for a sample garment. Without it the people involved with producing samples have no definite information as to what to do and how. Verbal instructions can be misunderstood or forgotten, so it is essential that the sample room staff have a written and illustrated specification of exactly what is required. Figure 14.2 shows an example of the design specification for a woman's outsize jacket, together with some items of information possibly needed for administration purposes.

What is fundamental to a design specification is not the amount of information it contains but the accuracy and relevance of the information which it communicates. Ideally, the specification should answer every practical question in advance.

FROM THE DESIGN DEPARTMENT

After a sample garment has been checked and approved by the designer, it is ready to be handed over to other related departments together with all the information required to prepare a costing. In the majority of factories, the design department is not expected to provide accurate and finalised costings for sample garments, but to collate and present a reliable basis for the costing clerk to work from.

There are a number of practical reasons why the design department is not the realistic place for garment costings, as explained below.

The preparation of garment costings requires people specialising in the subject and these people are not generally working members of the design team. Specialisation implies a specific area of expertise and both designers and costing clerks are experts in their respective fields. Therefore the most efficient results for the company are achieved when employees concentrate on what they do best and are not given extraneous tasks for which they have little working expertise.

The sample room cuts single size markers and whilst the sample cutter will attempt to be as economical as possible, a skilled marker planner will nearly always achieve better results. If the sample room pattern has been constructed on a CAD system, it can be easily transferred to the marker planner in the factory cutting room in order to obtain accurate figures regarding materials requirements. If manual methods are used, the factory's marker planner should be called in to check over the pattern arrangements made in the sample room before figures are finalised.

Figure14.2.

Design Specification

Season/Phase	Description	Size	Block Number	Designer	Pattern Cutter
Spring/2	Tailored Jacket	12	347	Katie	John

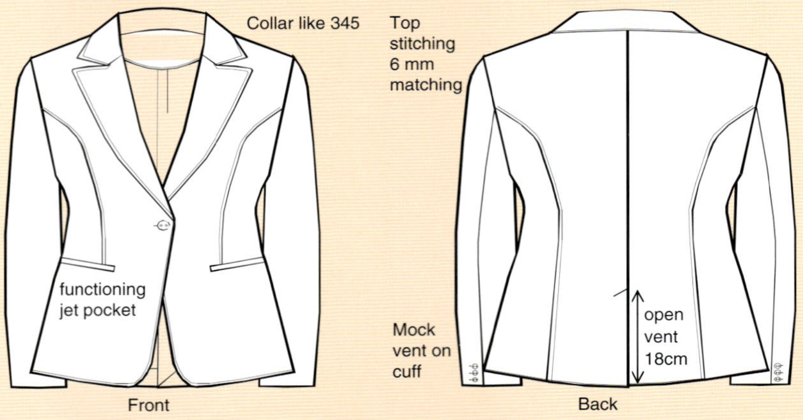

Collar like 345

Top stitching 6 mm matching

functioning jet pocket

Front

open vent 18cm

Mock vent on cuff

Back

Self

Supplier	Quality	Comp	Colour
Texall	6164	100% wool	14

Buttons

Supplier	Type	Size	Colour
Sprint	465	CF 50L	DTM
Sprint	465	Cuff 24L	DTM

Lining

Supplier	Quality	For	Colour
Linetex	551	Body	27
Gemtex	45	Sleeve	43

Interlinings

Supplier	Quality	For	Colour
Fusemat	388	Fronts	Charcoal
Fusemat	210	Collar Patch	Charcoal
Fusemat	408	Jet	Charcoal

Pads

Supplier	Type	Size
Pollster	1361	L

Labels

Label	Type	Position
Brand/Size	Gerlin	Back Neck
Composition	100% Wool	Left Side Seam
Care	Dry Clean Only	Left Side Seam

Special Instructions

1 x spare 50L button, 1 x spare button 24L to be in clear bag kimballed to care label

Check cloth shrinkage prior to cutting

Standard construction

120 Threads DTM self and linings

Reinforce jet pocket openings

Some companies, especially those producing for stock, calculate materials requirements on the basis of markers containing a fixed ratio of sizes. Again it is not practical for the sample room to become involved in this extensive and skilled work, so it is better left to the experts.

The price of materials and trimmings is often open to negotiation with suppliers, and the designer is not usually involved in this side of the business. The designer will have ordered sample materials knowing that the quoted prices are within the planned framework, but this price is not always the actual price which the company will pay.

Although sample garments are planned to be produced within a standard work-content framework, many deviations occur during their making up. The precise analysis of work-content and operations in order to establish labour costs is the work of a skilled clothing technician, even though the sample room could possibly provide an intelligent guesstimate.

Finally, it is in the best interests of a company to have "horses for courses" rather than a free-for-all situation.

Sample Summary Sheet

The sample room accrues a great deal of pertinent information concerning each sample from start to finish, and this information has to be communicated to people responsible for analysis and costing. It should be emphasised that this information is not a costing but rather a reasonably dependable basis from which a costing can be developed. For example purposes, the medium by which the information is communicated can be called a sample summary sheet (Figure 14.3). (The outsize jacket illustrated on the sample summary sheet in Figure 14.3 is the end product of that shown in the design specification in Figure 14.2.)

The objectives of this document are to provide other specialist functions in the company with a fairly accurate and comprehensive summary of what has been invested in a sample as regards materials, trimmings and labour. When the information on this sheet has been processed, it not only generates the garment costing but it also provides the basis for all the production and logistic planning concerned with a particular garment. Consequently, its compilation requires some punctilious work on the part of the design department.

The extent of the summary sheet is obviously dependent on the relative complexity of the garment category manufactured by the company, but the following are some typical examples of the items which could appear on this document:

(1) A sketch of the sample plus, when relevant, illustrations of any new or unique design features. It is not really necessary for this sketch to have the written content of the design specification.
(2) Each and every type of material and the quantities used for the sample have to be listed. If there have been difficulties with any particular material, this should be pointed out and the reasons stated. This is important because it

Figure14.3.

Sample Summary Sheet

Season/Phase	Description	Style Number	Market	Size Range	Sample Size
Spring/2	Tailored Jacket	BJ0114	Home	8,10,12,14,16,18,20,22	12

Front

Back

Item	Supplier	Qual	Quantity	Item	Buttons	Supplier	Type	Size	Quantity
Cloth	Texall	6164	1.6mtrs			Sprint	465	50L	1 + 1 spare
						Sprint	465	24L	6 + 1 spare

Figure 14.3. *Continued*

Lining	Linetex	551	1.30 mtrs
Fusibles	Fusemat	388	0.90 mtrs
	Fusemat	210	0.35 mtrs
	Fusemat	408	0.15 mtrs

Labels

Label	**Source**	**Format**	**Quantity**
Brand/size	Stock	Gerlin 4	1
Comp	Stock	100% wool	1
Care	Stock	Dry clean	1

Pads

Supplier	**Type**	**Size**
Pollster	1361	L

Construction	**Special Operations**	**Designer**
Standard	6 mm topstitching	Katie

Sewing Threads

120's DTM

Date 6-Nov

Comments:

Self shrinks 3.5% in warp direction.

might be necessary to change the material in order to prevent future problems with quality or in production processes.

(3) Every trimming used must be listed in the same detail as the materials. Nothing should be overlooked because each item, however small, is part of the logistics chain for production. Imagine the situation if the factory had to put hundreds of uncompleted garments aside not just because a needed item of trim had not been ordered, but even worse because no one even knew that the item was needed for the garments. So on the summary sheet every small item must be considered indispensable information.

(4) Full particulars of any outside services used, such as embroidery, must be recorded. If the provider of the service is new to the company, it helps to include the name to contact.

(5) Attention should be drawn to any special processes employed when making up the sample. This is important for the production department as it enables them to plan in advance rather than discover new special operations at the last minute.

(6) There are also a number of company procedures to observe, mainly concerned with garment identification. From an administrative point of view, this information is no less important than any other items on the sheet.

Product Life-cycle Management Software

All of these aspects of effective communication are aided by web based software that allows every element to be stored (in a suitable database structure) and managed/accessed by appropriate users in geographically dispersed locations through the connectivity of the World Wide Web. PLM software is the natural evolution of Product Data Management (PDM) systems that were originally used in house to manage all the relevant information for each design development and the subsequent production of that garment.

CHAPTER 15

Management/Leadership and Organisation

Although at first glance it might seem a little odd to discuss management in a book of this nature, management is essential for all organised activity, and regardless of size the design department is no exception. Although it may not be expressed explicitly, the formal process whereby somebody is appointed to be in charge of the department means that for all practical purposes this person is the manager. They have to operate the department with all that the word *management* involves within the context of a traditional hierarchical structure. As designers are usually selected for this position, they have to understand something about the principles of management in order to contribute to the professional performance of the department.

The extent of the managerial activities involved is very much dependent on the sizes of the design and sample sections and the organisation of the working relationship between them. In a small factory where there might be only five or six people concerned with design and sample production, they could all probably work comfortably together in one large room. The designer in charge can see everything that is going on and managing the operation of a unit this size is more hands-on than through remote control. Obviously the elements of organisation, planning and control have to be used but they are relatively simple to apply.

On the other hand a large scale manufacturer of fashion wear would operate a big design department which needs more space and personnel and a great deal of applied management skills. In a set-up of this nature, where the design department is responsible for the production of a large quantity of sample garments, the total operation would probably be divided into two groups; the design section and the sample room.

Design Section

This group works closely with the marketing department and would be responsible for all the design and design related activities, plus the in-process and final approval of samples. If the company produces a range of different garment types, the design section could be subdivided into design groups specialising in one type of garment. Each of these groups would comprise designers, stylists, pattern cutters, etc, and would be headed by an appropriate member of the team. The heads of these teams would receive their design briefings from the department's manager or manageress who would also give the final approval to the samples produced by each group.

Sample Room

This is where the sample garments are cut, made and finished, and in a large scale operation this department would require very active management to ensure its effective operation. Normally this department would be managed by a person who has had extensive practical experience with the garments produced by the company and who also knows and can interpret the idiosyncrasies of each designer. The sample room supervisor would work in close coordination with the design room staff and would be accountable to the manager or manageress of the department.

THE PRINCIPLES

How the design and sample sections are organised and managed is mainly a question of scale, but whatever the circumstances the same principles are applicable and these include the following aspects.

Management

Management is often described in terms of techniques, formulae and procedures. While these are pertinent to sophisticated industrial and commercial environments, the management of the design department is a far less complex situation. At this level management is a relatively simple operation which combines a social and systematic approach because decisions are implemented by people working according to the manager's evaluation of the facts.

For the design department management can be considered the systematic planning and control of activities within an organised framework, which enables the personnel to work productively and happily.

Organisation

All groups of people working together require an organisational structure in order to form them into a complete and functioning unit. Due to the nature of its work, the design department has no need for a strictly prescribed organisation; more of a "free-wheeling" but responsible approach is appropriate. Every member of the department has to be aware of their specific operational responsibilities, how far they can go in any given situation and to whom they are accountable.

Apart from creating a known and structured working environment, good organisation also provides people with a feeling of security in the sense of belonging to a group and participating in a united effort.

Planning and Control

Planning is concerned with setting realistic objectives and providing the means to achieve them, whilst control establishes the criteria and procedures needed to check the progress and results of what has been planned. For the design department the functions of planning and control are indispensable, because without them nobody knows exactly what to do, when to do it and with what to do it. If planning is nonexistent, control procedures are worthless because there are no pre-determined criteria for comparison.

Even the smallest design department has to plan its work in advance so that sample collections will be available for the marketing department by the right date. Time is an important factor in the production of sample garments and collection completion dates determine priorities and objectives. Therefore a small department which plans its work according to time alone is automatically provided with a rudimentary but practical method of global control.

The larger design department requires a more detailed form of planning and control due to the number of people working at different tasks on numerous sample garments. If the company has a substantial export business, planning is of paramount importance because the department has to produce collections for different seasons parallel to those being produced for their home market and that of other countries. A department of this size is literally a sample factory and it has to employ similar planning and control techniques to those used by a small industrial production unit.

However, there is a difference between the scales of planning and control for a factory and for a design department. In a factory these two functions are built around bulk work and the performance of groups, whereas in a design department single garments are the unit of production and most of the work is performed by individuals.

Coordination

The objectives of coordination are to ensure a balanced and suitable allocation of tasks between all the people directly involved with designing and producing sample garments. To a great extent coordination is based on recorded data or the accumulated experience of what people are capable of doing during a specific time. This knowledge has to be applied when planning a balanced work flow between:

- Designers and stylists.
- Pattern cutters.
- Sample cutters.
- Sample production personnel.
- Inspection personnel.

Approved designs are handed over to pattern cutters for refinement and engineering (but it should be clear that a competent designer has good knowledge of pattern cutting techniques), each of whom might have unique areas of expertise. Consequently the allocation of designs to the pattern cutters has to take into account the general and specific capabilities and work rate of each one so that the load is spread equitably. When patterns are completed, the next stage is cutting and this requires two elements of coordination:

(1) That all the materials and trimmings needed for samples are on hand when they are due to be cut.
(2) That the department has sufficient sample cutters to cope with the planned daily quantity.

The sewing, pressing, finishing and inspection of samples are carried out by a group of employees with a known individual and group capability often in excess of that of the average production operative. These capabilities have to be carefully balanced so that each individual can make an effective contribution to the group's overall performance.

The coordination of activities is central to the competent operation of the design department. Working in a stop-start situation caused by a lack of coordination is not particularly conducive to efficiency and motivation.

Personnel

As a group the people in the design department need to be versatile specialists because of the dynamics of the fashion business. Designers are continually developing designs in new materials, and pattern cutters have to cope with an extremely high rate of style changes. The sample room operators do not have a learning period for each new sample but have to manage with an explanation and then produce a first-time garment in the shortest possible time.

This situation demands a high level of professionalism from everyone involved, and in this context professionalism means:

(1) That the person is a fully trained and experienced expert in his or her field of specialisation.
(2) That the person has a professional approach to their work and can operate independently and conscientiously without the need for constant supervision and direction.

The selection of personnel is an exacting process because, regardless of the manager's own abilities, a manager will ultimately only be as good as the people working for him/her.

Motivation

Apart from being a place of business, a company is also a working day social environment and managers have to possess and apply social skills in addition to their other management skills. Motivation has long been recognised as an important tool of management and without it a group of employees will never really be fused into a smoothly working team making a united effort. Obviously motivation in itself will not create high performance levels if people lack the appropriate experience and/or qualifications. But if they have ability and are well trained, motivation will significantly enhance both individual and collective levels of performance.

When people are treated fairly and are well motivated, they find a form of social anchorage in their work place and this makes an important contribution to the level of their participation. This can only be created by management who set a personal example and have an active awareness of the value of motivation.

THE PRACTICE OF MANAGEMENT

The extent of managerial activities in the design department is relative to its size, but whatever its size the department does have to be managed. Some practical pointers are given below.

Responsibility and Authority

When a person is appointed to manage the department, he or she is automatically made accountable for the results. This is responsibility, but this alone is insufficient for effective management if the same person is not given the equivalent scale of authority. In other words, if the manager has the full responsibility for running the department, then he or she has to be vested with the full authority to act according to the scope and terms of the responsibility.

Administration

There are usually many administrative procedures which have to be dealt with in the day-to-day work of a manager. Some of these are part of the company's internal administrative systems, whilst many others are directly concerned with personnel.

Internal systems will only work well if they are continually updated with accurate information, so the manager has a clear responsibility in this direction. Where people are concerned, administrative details should be attended to correctly and promptly because dealing with people's problems is part of the human relations network within the department.

Advancement

Many people working in the department have professional ambitions, and often the department has similar ambitions for the same people. When the ambitions are the same on both sides, the manager has a responsibility to realise them as well as possible.

Whether it concerns a raise in salary, promotion or a transfer to another type of work, if the change is justified it should be effected at the most propitious time. An employee who has to wait an unreasonable length of time for a decision is apt to become a frustrated employee, with all the associated negative aspects. It does much for the general morale in the department if the personnel know that ability and application will be recognised and rewarded.

Training

Due to changing demands, it is not always possible to keep an employee continuously on the work to which he or she is accustomed. Consequently the manager needs to consider the possibility of training some members of staff to perform other operations. Given sufficient experience with their new operations, these people can always help out when the pressure is on, apart from being a reserve in the event of absences. The production of sample garments requires a high level of versatility and the investment in developing additional proficiencies is always worthwhile.

Planning and Control

These two inseparable activities are the tools by which management sets objectives and is enabled to verify results. It is essential that all the work of the design department is planned in advance and that control systems are set up in order

Table 15.1.

Skirt Design Programme							
Season: Winter				**Phase: 1**		**Completion: 20/6**	
Designer	**Market/ Customer**	**Cost price range**	**Core samples**				**Total**
Jackie	home	£18–20	4104	4106	4107	/	16
Anne	home	£22–25	4111	4116	4118	4120	15
Anne	home/D&B	£18–20	4121	4124	4127	/	12
Jackie	home/Adnac	£20–22	4103	4108	4112	4122	12
Janet	USA/WM	$35–40	4103	4104	4411	4118	12
Janet	Germany/Bos	€45–50	4104	4111	4126	4130	15
						Total	**82**

that the status and progress of the plans can be evaluated. Some examples are given below.

Design Programme

The example of a design programme in Table 15.1 is for a company producing skirts and it covers the various collections required for the first phase of the forthcoming winter season (although designs may be produced in multiple "drops" throughout a year it is still useful to think in terms of seasons). The programme works as follows.

The allocation of collections between the designers involved is based on the individual designer's experience with a particular market and/or customer and the core samples developed by the same designer. Each collection has a defined cost price range and the designers have to select materials and plan work content so that their samples fall within these limits. The core samples selected as the basis for each collection are those considered most suitable for a particular market or customer, and when appropriate the same core sample can be used more than once.

Production Planning

Table 15.2 shows an example of a production planning and control system. The principles of its operation are as follows.

It sets out in detail the planned deliveries of the sample room to the marketing department during one working week. The week itself is denoted by the international week numbering system and the matching dates. In this example,

Table 15.2.

		Sample Production Plan				
Week	Date	**Planned** **Deliveries**	Jackets	Coats		Total
18	16/4 - 20/4		20	15		35

Style No.	Gmt	Cut	Sew	Pressed	Inspected	Approved	Delivered
6164	jkt	11-Apr	12-Apr	13-Apr	13-Apr	13-Apr	16-Apr
6166	jkt	10-Apr	11-Apr	12-Apr	13-Apr	13-Apr	16-Apr
5404	coat	10-Apr	11-Apr	12-Apr	13-Apr	13-Apr	16-Apr
5405	coat	10-Apr	11-Apr	12-Apr	13-Apr	16-Apr	16-Apr
5406	coat	11-Apr	12-Apr	13-Apr	16-Apr	16-Apr	16-Apr
6167	jkt	11-Apr	12-Apr	13-Apr	16-Apr	16-Apr	17-Apr
6169	jkt	11-Apr	12-Apr	13-Apr	16-Apr	16-Apr	17-Apr
5408	coat	11-Apr	12-Apr	13-Apr	16-Apr	16-Apr	17-Apr
5410	coat	11-Apr	12-Apr	13-Apr	16-Apr	17-Apr	17-Apr
6168	jkt	12-Apr	13-Apr	16-Apr	17-Apr	17-Apr	17-Apr
5411	coat	12-Apr	13-Apr	16-Apr	17-Apr	17-Apr	17-Apr
6170	jkt	12-Apr	13-Apr	16-Apr			

	Daily and Weekly Summary									
Date	16-Apr		17-Apr		18-Apr		19-Apr		20-Apr	
Garment	jkts.	coats	jkts.	coats	jkts.	coats	jkts.	coats	jkts.	coats
Delivery	3	3	4	3	4	4	5	3	4	4
To Date	3	3	7	6	11	10	16	13	20	17

sample garments take four to five days (throughput time) to produce; some of the planned deliveries were commenced during the previous week and will be completed in the current week. The progress of each garment is controlled by entering the date when a key operation of its production is completed. These dates are obtained from the daily work sheets (see Table 15.3) completed by

Table 15.3.

			Daily Worksheet			
Name	**Alison**	**No.**	**2208**	**Job**	**cutter**	
			Quantities			
Style No.	**Gmt.**	**top cloth**	**direction**	**lining**	**fusible int.**	
6184	skirt	0.7	>	0.65	Band	
6185	skirt	0.75	<>		Band	
6186	skirt	0.7	<>	0.65	Band	
4534	jkt	1.15	>	0.75	Band + 10cm	
4536	jkt	1.1	<>		Band + 10cm	
4537	jkt	1.1	>		Band + 10cm	
Jkts: /	Skirts 3	Trs 3	Total	Total	6	

operators or supervisors. The lower part of Table 15.2 shows a summary of the daily and cumulative results. This system provides management with detailed and up-to-date information regarding sample production.

Reporting

The example of a daily work sheet shown in Table 15.3 is that for a sample cutter who records details of the garments cut and such additional information as is required. Other operators also use similar types of forms and all of these are used to control the progress of each garment during its production in the sample room.

Control Systems

Whatever reporting method is used, the most important factor is the practical relevance of the information conveyed by the report. The real bottom line for the manager is not how many buttonholes were sewn yesterday but the number of sample garments delivered to the marketing department the previous day. In addition, the manager also requires information regarding the exact status of all the samples planned to be produced during a specific period. This information is essential because if the manager sees or anticipates possible bottle-necks, remedial action can be taken before major problems occur. Moreover, this information is vital when bulk production begins in order to pre-manage potential problems.

A reporting system has to be selective regarding the type and extent of information it reports. Too much irrelevant information wastes people's time and too little of the key information is inconclusive. So for a report to be effective, it has to be short and to the point. Conventional reporting systems work on a daily basis and the accumulated information can be summarised for or by the manager and also posted on a prominently displayed wall chart for all members of the staff to see.

FURTHER READING

Carr, H. and Pomeroy, J. (1992) *Fashion Design and Product Development*. Blackwell Science, Oxford.

Cooklin, G. (1989) *Fusing Technology*. The Textile Institute, Manchester.

Cooklin, G. (1996) *Introduction to Clothing Manufacture*, 2nd edn. Blackwell Science, Oxford.

Cooklin, G., Hayes, S. and McLoughlin, J. (2006) *Introduction to Clothing Manufacture*, 2nd edn. Blackwell Publishing, Oxford.

Cooper, G.R. (1985) *The Sewing Machine – Its Invention and Development*, 2nd edn. Smithsonian Press, Washington.

Friend, R.L. (1977) *Sewing Room Technical Handbook*. HATRA, The Research Centre for Knitting, Dyeing and Making-up, Nottingham.

Hall, A.J. (1965) *The Standard Handbook of Textiles*, 5th edn. Temple Press Books, London.

Hudson, P.B. (1989) *Guide to Apparel Manufacturing*. Media Inc., Greensboro, North Carolina.

Jeffrey, M. and Evans, N. (2011) *Costing for the fashion industry*. Berg: Oxford and New York.

Lowe, J. and Lowcock, P.D. (1986) *An Approach to Quality Control in the Clothing Industry*. Emraine Publications, Ware, Herts.

Lyle, O. (1960) *The Efficient Use of Steam*. HMSO, London.

Trautman, J.E. (1979) *Materials Utilisation in the Apparel Industry*. Apparel Research Foundation, Arlington.

Solinger, J. (1988) Apparel Manufacturing Handbook, 2nd edn. Bobbin Blenheim, Columbia, South Carolina.

Tylor, D.J. (ed) (2008). *Carr & Latham's Technology of Clothing Manufacture*, 4th edn. Blackwell: Oxford.

COMPANY PUBLICATIONS

How to Lay Checks. Bullmerwerk GmbH, Mehrstetten, Germany.

The Technology of Thread and Seams. Coats Ltd, Enderby, Leicester.

Fusing Without Risk. Kannegiesser GmbH, Vlotho, Germany.

INDEX